GCSE English AQA Anthology

The Study Guide

Poems from Different Cultures

AQA A Specification — Higher Level

This book is a step-by-step guide to becoming an expert on the Anthology part of your GCSE English exam.

It's got everything you need to know — annotated poems, exam themes and worked essays.

It's ideal for use as a classroom study book or a revision guide.

CONTENTS

How to Use This Book 1

Section One — The Poems

Poems from Different Cultures: Cluster 1
Limbo 2
Nothing's Changed 4
Island Man 6
Blessing 8
Two Scavengers in a Truck 10
Night of the Scorpion 12
Vultures 14
What Were They Like? 16

Poems from Different Cultures: Cluster 2
Search For My Tongue 18
Unrelated Incidents 20
Half-Caste 22
Love After Love 24
This Room 26
Presents from my Aunts in Pakistan 28
Not my Business 30
Hurricane Hits England 32

Section Two — The Themes

Identity 34
Politics 35
Change 36
People 37
First Person 38
Specific Cultural References 39
Description 40
Metaphor 41
Unusual Presentation 42
Non-Standard English 43
Particular Places 44
Two Cultures 45
Universal Ideas 46
Traditions 47

Section Three — How to Answer the Question

Sample Essay and Exam Method: Identity 48
Sample Essay and Exam Method: Description 50
Sample Essay and Exam Method: Politics 52
Sample Essay and Exam Method: People 54

Glossary 56
Index 58

Published by Coordination Group Publications Ltd.

Contributors:
Charley Darbishire, Roland Haynes, Kate Houghton,
Katherine Reed, Edward Robinson and Elisabeth Sanderson

With thanks to Sue Hirst and Kate Redmond for the proofreading.

ISBN: 1-84146-696-4

Groovy website: www.cgpbooks.co.uk

Jolly bits of clipart from CorelDRAW

Printed by Elanders Hindson, Newcastle upon Tyne.

Text, design, layout and original illustrations © Coordination Group Publications Ltd. 2004
All rights reserved.

How To Use This Book

This book will help you do better in your GCSE English Anthology Exam. It's full of straightforward ways of getting extra marks. Start by asking your teacher which poems and themes you need to study: some schools get you to study all of them, others pick out certain ones.

There are Three Sections in this book

Section One is all about the Poems

There are two pages about each poem. This is what the pages look like:

The poem is on the left hand page, along with other useful features:

- Important or tricky bits of the poem are highlighted and explained.
- Difficult words are defined in the poem dictionary at the bottom.
- There's a nice picture of the poet and some info about their life.

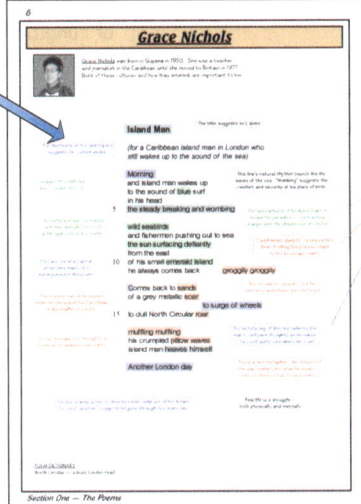

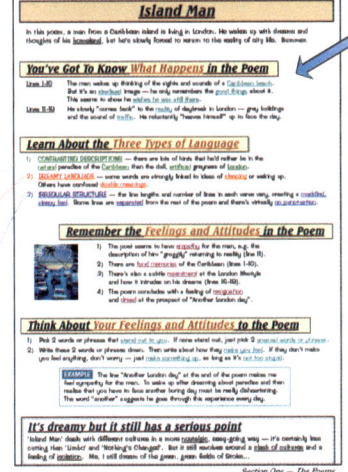

On the right hand page there are notes about the poem. They talk about:

- What happens in the poem.
- The language the poet uses.
- The feelings of the poet.
- A bit that will help you to decide what you think of the poem.

Read through the pages on the poems you've been told to study. When you've read about each poem, shut the book and write out as much as you can remember. See what you left out, then do it again. It's boring, but a great way to learn.

Section Two is about the Themes

In the exam, you'll have to compare how two poems relate to one of the themes. There's a page about each of the main themes that might come up in Section Two. The pages tell you which poems use each theme and how different poets treat the same theme. Read it, understand it and learn it.

Section Three is About Preparing for Your Exam

Section Three is about the CGP Five-Step Method™ which helps you to write essays that get good marks.

The pages on the left explain the CGP Five-Step Method of answering exam questions.

This method helps you use the information you learn in Sections One and Two to write good essays.

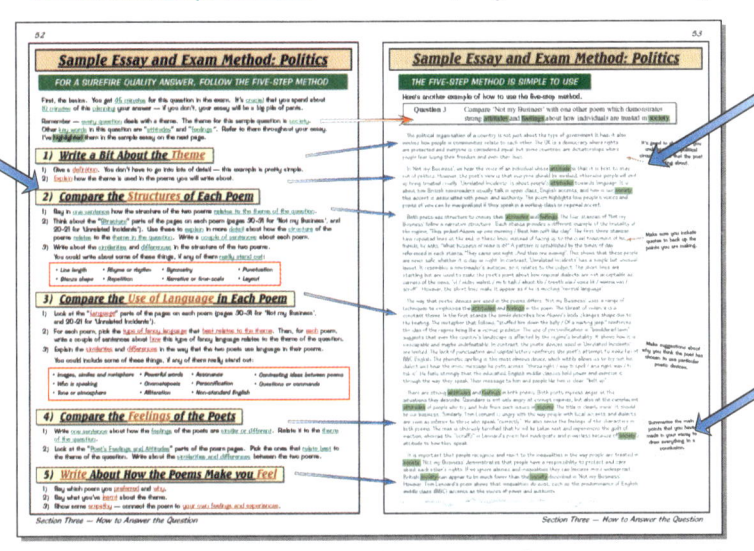

The pages on the right have sample exam essay answers to show you what you're aiming for.

The little boxes at the side are tips on how you can get extra marks in the Exam.

Write some essays using the Five-Step Method. Use the exam-style questions in the CGP Anthology Workbook, if you have it, or ask your teacher for some practice questions. You get 45 minutes to answer the 'Poetry from Different Cultures' question in the Exam, so practise doing some timed essays.

THIS IS A FLAP.
FOLD THIS PAGE OUT.

How To Use This Book

This book will help you do better in your GCSE English Anthology Exam. It's full of straightforward ways of getting extra marks. Start by asking your teacher which poems and themes you need to study: some schools get you to study all of them, others pick out certain ones.

There are Three Sections in this book

Section One is all about the Poems

There are two pages about each poem. This is what the pages look like:

The poem is on the left hand page, along with other useful features:

- Important or tricky bits of the poem are highlighted and explained.
- Difficult words are defined in the poem dictionary at the bottom.
- There's a nice picture of the poet and some info about their life.

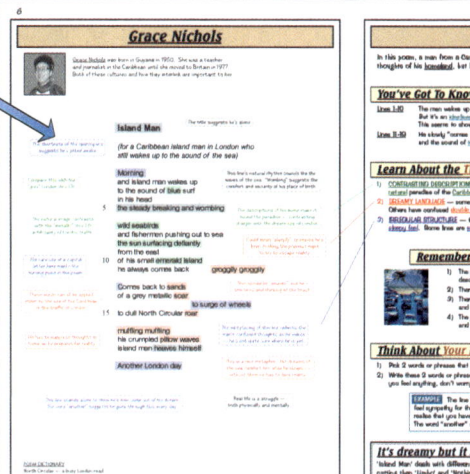

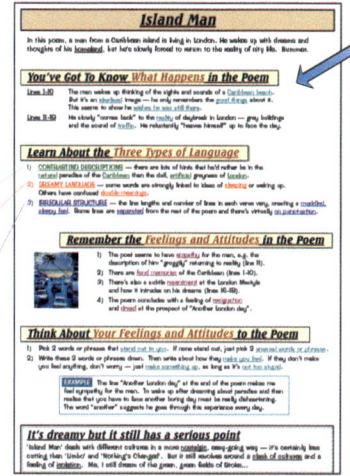

On the right hand page there are notes about the poem. They talk about:

- What happens in the poem.
- The language the poet uses.
- The feelings of the poet.
- A bit that will help you to decide what you think of the poem.

Read through the pages on the poems you've been told to study. When you've read about each poem, shut the book and write out as much as you can remember. See what you left out, then do it again. It's boring, but a great way to learn.

Section Two is about the Themes

In the exam, you'll have to compare how two poems relate to one of the themes. There's a page about each of the main themes that might come up in Section Two. The pages tell you which poems use each theme and how different poets treat the same theme. Read it, understand it and learn it.

Section Three is About Preparing for Your Exam

Section Three is about the CGP Five-Step Method™ which helps you to write essays that get good marks.

The pages on the left explain the CGP Five-Step Method of answering exam questions.

This method helps you use the information you learn in Sections One and Two to write good essays.

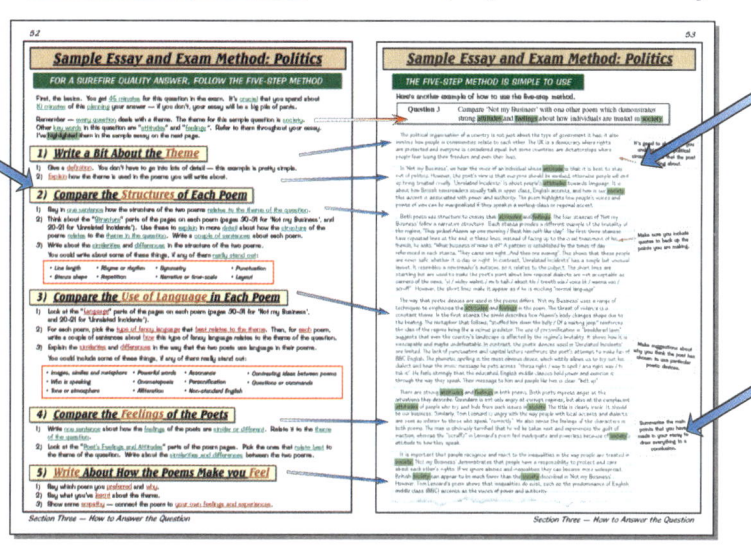

The pages on the right have sample exam essay answers to show you what you're aiming for.

The little boxes at the side are tips on how you can get extra marks in the Exam.

Write some essays using the Five-Step Method. Use the exam-style questions in the CGP Anthology Workbook, if you have it, or ask your teacher for some practice questions. You get 45 minutes to answer the 'Poetry from Different Cultures' question in the Exam, so practise doing some timed essays.

Edward Kamau Brathwaite

Use of first person engages the reader and makes them sympathetic.

This suggests the low ceilings of the decks of the ship.

Repetition of these lines emphasises the harshness of conditions on the ship.

One-syllable words and long vowel sounds make this line feel slow and deliberate.

Before rising out of slavery, he sinks right to the bottom.

The drum offers hope — it's like a friend to him.

This line is the turning point of the poem — darkness is replaced by light.

New hope — he's lifted out of the darkness.

Here he finally ascends out of the misery of slavery.

The slow three step beat suggests a weary but steady emergence from slavery, and also the end of the dance.

This fiery image could suggest he's reached hell and that his time in limbo is over.

The full stop at the end — the only one in the poem — represents the end of the dance, of the voyage, and perhaps his life.

> knees spread wide
> and the water is hiding
>
> 30 limbo
> limbo like me
>
> knees spread wide
> and the dark ground is under me
>
> 35 down
> down
> down
> and the drummer is calling me
>
> limbo
> limbo like me
>
> 40 sun coming up
> and the drummers are praising me
>
> out of the dark
> and the dumb gods are raising me
>
> up
> 45 up
> up
> and the music is saving me
>
> hot
> 50 slow
> step
> on the burning ground.

© Edward Kamau Brathwaite 'Limbo' from *The Arrivants: A New World Trilogy* (OUP, 1973), reprinted by permission of Oxford University Press.

POEM DICTIONARY
Limbo has several meanings —
1. The West Indian dance, crouching backwards to pass under a horizontal stick — said to have originated from the memories of travelling in the cramped decks of the slave ships
2. An imaginary place for the unwanted or forgotten
3. In Christianity, a place where infants who die before baptism go — a place of uncertainty, as they don't know if they're going to heaven or hell

Section One — The Poems

Section One — The Poems

Edward Kamau Brathwaite

Edward Kamau Brathwaite was born in 1930 in Barbados in the West Indies. He's a poet and historian, and he's interested in links between slave nations and their African origins.

Limbo

And limbo stick is the silence in front of me
limbo

limbo
limbo like me
5   limbo
limbo like me

long dark night is the silence in front of me
limbo
limbo like me

10   stick hit sound
and the ship like it ready

stick hit sound
and the dark still steady

limbo
15   limbo like me

long dark deck and the water surrounding me
long dark deck and the silence is over me

limbo
limbo like me

20   stick is the whip
and the dark deck is slavery

stick is the whip
and the dark deck is slavery

limbo
25   limbo like me

drum stick knock
and the darkness is over me

Annotations:

- These lines set up the limbo rhythm which is repeated throughout the poem.
- The silence is like a threat or a danger sign.
- The plodding rhythm of this line adds to the repetitive feel.
- The slave ship that took the African slaves to the Caribbean.
- The strong alliteration adds to the impact of the beating of the slaves.
- This suggests the start of the voyage.
- The words "deck" and "dark" are repeated again in lines 21 and 23.
- "Stick" has a double meaning — the stick the slaves were beaten with, and the limbo pole.
- Very similar lines suggest he's completely trapped.
- Darkness symbolises the despair of slavery.
- The hard consonant sounds of these words add to the regular, rhythmic feel. These words are also onomatopoeic.

THIS IS A FLAP.
FOLD THIS PAGE OUT.

Limbo

This poem uses the limbo dance as an extended metaphor. The poet uses it to describe the story of African people being transported as human cargo to the Caribbean colonies to work as slaves. So understandably, it's not a barrel of laughs.

You've Got To Know What Happens in the Poem

Lines 1-19   The poem begins in the midst of slavery. Two main themes are introduced — the limbo dance, and the voyage of the slave ship.

Lines 20-36   The middle of the poem is the middle of the voyage, right under the stick or limbo pole.

Lines 37-51   In the final section, the poet sees an end to the suffering. He comes "out of the dark" at last — although where he ends up is unclear.

Learn About the Four Types of Language

1) **REFERENCES TO SLAVERY** — this is the main theme. The journey of the first African slaves is linked to the poet's individual life. The past and present are difficult to separate.

2) **REPETITION** — the lines "limbo/limbo like me" are repeated throughout the poem. Some lines are repeated with minor differences, e.g. lines 16 and 17, lines 41 and 43.

3) **METAPHORICAL LANGUAGE** — descriptions of darkness and the slave ship are used to stress the living hell of slavery. The voyage of the ship is used as a metaphor for the long-term plight of generations of slaves.

4) **RHYTHM** — the beat of the drum on the ship emphasises the monotony and relentlessness of slave labour. Also, the tribal beat of the limbo dance recalls the slaves' African roots.

Remember the Feelings and Attitudes in the Poem

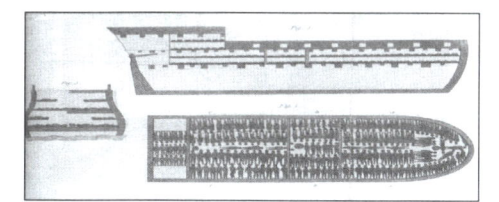

Plan of a slave ship

1) He's angry at the conditions on the cramped slave ship and the cruelty the slaves have suffered (e.g. line 20).
2) But he admires the strength and resolve of the slaves.
3) He celebrates the slaves' past — and their survival (line 47).

> We experience a mixture of emotions in 'Limbo' — we feel the slaves' fear and suffering but also their joy in survival.

Think About Your Feelings and Attitudes to the Poem

1) Pick 2 words or phrases that stand out to you. If none stand out, just pick 2 unusual words or phrases.
2) Write these 2 words or phrases down. Then write about how they make you feel. If they don't make you feel anything, don't worry — just make something up, as long as it's not too stupid.

> **EXAMPLE** On line 41, the poet says "The drummers are praising me". Up to this point, the dance has been symbolic of the monotony of slave life, but it seems to me that the music is now a positive thing. I think the drummers are his African ancestors, helping him out of the hell of slavery.

Talk about the effect of the poem as a whole

The poem is one long sentence. This helps to create the feel of a continuous dance, and the seemingly never-ending suffering of the slaves. Having "and" as the first word suggests this isn't the start of the suffering — it's been going on for generations.

Section One — The Poems

Tatamkhulu Afrika

> There's no official segregation, but the feeling of inequality lives on.

25 No sign says it is:
    but we know where we belong.

> He's an outsider to the luxury of life as a white person.

    I press my nose
    to the clear panes, know,
    before I see them, there will be
30 crushed ice white glass,
    linen falls,
    the single rose.

> Here the glass represents the whites drinking in the splendour of the inn.

> The inn and the cafe are close to each other, but completely separate.

    Down the road,
    working man's cafe sells
35 bunny chows.
    Take it with you, eat
    it at a plastic table's top,
    wipe your fingers on your jeans,
    spit a little on the floor:
40 it's in the bone.

> The cafe has basic food and plastic tables — compare this to the white people's inn (21-22).

> This could mean that black people have lived like this for so long that it now seems natural.

    I back from the glass,
    boy again,
    leaving small mean O
    of small, mean mouth.
45 Hands burn
    for a stone, a bomb,
    to shiver down the glass.
    Nothing's changed.

> The mark left by his mouth on the glass.

> Language shows that the man feels rejected.

> "Boy" is a South African word, often insulting, for a black male of any age. It also reminds him that it was the same when he was a child as it is now.

> He's angry and wants to take action.

> i.e. remove the barrier between black and white.

> The poem concludes on a negative note — he doesn't see any difference in post-apartheid South Africa. This makes him very angry.

POEM DICTIONARY
amiable — likeable / friendly
incipient — developing, just starting
Port Jackson trees — large pine trees
haute cuisine — high-class, expensive food
bunny chows — cheap food for the poor

Section One — The Poems

Tatamkhulu Afrika

Tatamkhulu Afrika (1920-2002) was born in Egypt but raised as a white South African. When apartheid was introduced, he refused to be classed as a "superior" white, and moved to District Six in Cape Town. He joined the African National Congress (ANC) and was a political prisoner because of his fight against apartheid.

Nothing's Changed

Small round hard stones click
under my heels,
seeding grasses thrust
bearded seeds
5   into trouser cuffs, cans,
trodden on, crunch
in tall, purple-flowering,
amiable weeds.

District Six.
10 No board says it is:
but my feet know,
and my hands,
and the skin about my bones,
and the soft labouring of my lungs,
15 and the hot, white, inwards turning
anger of my eyes.

Brash with glass,
name flaring like a flag,
it squats
20 in the grass and weeds,
incipient Port Jackson trees:
new, up-market, haute cuisine,
guard at the gatepost,
whites only inn.

Annotations:
- There's a wild and neglected feel to the area.
- Alliteration and one-syllable words make the tone snappy and hard hitting.
- Onomatopoeia creates a harsh, bitter mood.
- He prefers the weeds which belong in the area to the splendour of the newly planted trees (line 21) by the hotel.
- The recognition is physical.
- Suggests he's led a hard life.
- The repetition of "and" shows the poet's rising anger.
- He can't express his anger and frustration.
- A barrier keeping him out. He can see how the whites live but can't enter.
- The inn stands for the arrogance of the system.
- This simile shows the proud and insulting dominance of the inn — it seems to be taunting him.
- An ugly word, which suggests the inn doesn't belong there.
- The new inn, with posh food, contrasts sharply with the black people's cafe (34-39).
- Presumably there to keep black people out.

Section One — The Poems

THIS IS A FLAP.
FOLD THIS PAGE OUT.

Nothing's Changed

In this poem, the poet goes back to District Six. When he lived there it was a mixed-race area, but when apartheid was introduced in South Africa, it became a "whites only" area. Now, under Nelson Mandela's government, it's supposedly mixed again — but Afrika sees little difference.

You've Got To Know What Happens in the Poem

Lines 1-16   He describes his return to District Six. He says that, even though the old sign is gone, his senses tell him where he is — "my feet know / and my hands" (lines 11-12).

Lines 17-32   This section's about the inn. The inn represents the reality — blacks and whites still don't mix. It's clear that the inn is for white people only.

Line 33-48   He thinks about the cheap cafe "down the road". It's very different from the inn. In the final four lines, he says he wants to destroy the inn.

Learn About the Three Types of Language

1) **HARSHNESS and BITTERNESS** — he's angry at the inequality, and uses harsh-sounding words. They're often one-syllable words, with alliteration and onomatopoeia adding to the harsh feel.

2) **METAPHORICAL LANGUAGE** — the glass of the inn becomes a metaphor for apartheid. The inn represents the dominance and arrogance of the white people.

3) **COMPARISONS** — the differences between the lives of white and black people give you loads to talk about. Keep an eye out for comparisons split between different verses, e.g. the inn and the cafe.

Remember the Feelings and Attitudes in the Poem

1) There's the physical recognition of the poet's home district (lines 9-16).
2) But this is tinged with anger at its neglected state, and at the racial inequality that still exists (e.g. line 26).
3) There's bitterness and resentment in his contrasting descriptions of the white people's inn (lines 17-32) and the black people's cafe (lines 33-40).
4) This turns to violent feelings at the end of the poem, when he wants to "shiver down the glass" of the whites only inn (lines 45-47).

Nelson Mandela

Think About Your Feelings and Attitudes to the Poem

1) Pick 2 words or phrases that stand out to you. If none stand out, just pick 2 unusual words or phrases.
2) Write these 2 words or phrases down. Then write about how they make you feel. If they don't make you feel anything, don't worry — just make something up, as long as it's not too stupid.

> **EXAMPLE**   When the poet says, "We know where we belong," it makes me feel angry. Apartheid is supposed to be gone, yet, because of his race, the poet is all too aware of the inequalities that still exist. He's made to feel inferior to white people.

Show you know about the subject

The poet's opinion about South Africa is pretty clear cut — so you need to go into a bit more detail than just saying "he reckons it's the same as when apartheid was around". And if you can relate a few points about apartheid or Nelson Mandela to the poem, you'll really wow mean old Mr Examiner.

Grace Nichols

Grace Nichols was born in Guyana in 1950. She was a teacher and journalist in the Caribbean until she moved to Britain in 1977. Both of these cultures and how they interlink are important to her.

© Sheila Geraghty

Island Man

The title suggests he's alone.

(for a Caribbean island man in London who still wakes up to the sound of the sea)

The shortness of the opening line suggests he's jolted awake.

Morning
and island man wakes up
to the sound of blue surf
in his head
5   the steady breaking and womubing

This line's natural rhythm sounds like the waves of the sea. "Womubing" suggests the comfort and security of his place of birth.

Compare this with the "grey" London (line 13).

The natural image contrasts with the "metallic" (line 13) artificiality of London traffic.

wild seabirds
and fishermen pushing out to sea
the sun surfacing defiantly
from the east
10   of his small emerald island
he always comes back   groggily groggily

The descriptions of his home make it sound like paradise — contrasting sharply with the dreariness of London.

Could mean "sleepily", or maybe he's been drinking the previous night to try to escape reality.

The rare use of a capital letter here marks the turning point in the poem.

Comes back to sands
of a grey metallic soar
             to surge of wheels
15   to dull North Circular roar

This should be "sounds", but he's still tired and thinking of the beach.

These words can all be applied either to the sea of the Caribbean, or the traffic of London.

muffling muffling
his crumpled pillow waves
island man heaves himself

The odd placing of this line reflects the man's confused thoughts as he wakes — he's not quite sure where he is yet.

He has to suppress thoughts of home as he prepares for reality.

Another London day

This is a nice metaphor. His dreams of the sea comfort him while he sleeps — without them he has to face reality.

This line stands alone to show he's now come out of his dream. The word "another" suggests he goes through this every day.

Real life is a struggle — both physically and mentally.

POEM DICTIONARY
North Circular — a busy London road

Section One — The Poems

Island Man

In this poem, a man from a Caribbean island is living in London. He wakes up with dreams and thoughts of his homeland, but he's slowly forced to return to the reality of city life. Bummer.

You've Got To Know What Happens in the Poem

Lines 1-10 — The man wakes up thinking of the sights and sounds of a Caribbean beach. But it's an idealised image — he only remembers the good things about it. This seems to show he wishes he was still there.

Lines 11-19 — He slowly "comes back" to the reality of daybreak in London — grey buildings and the sound of traffic. He reluctantly "heaves himself" up to face the day.

Learn About the Three Types of Language

1) **CONTRASTING DESCRIPTIONS** — there are lots of hints that he'd rather be in the natural paradise of the Caribbean than the dull, artificial greyness of London.

2) **DREAMY LANGUAGE** — some words are strongly linked to ideas of sleeping or waking up. Others have confused double meanings.

3) **IRREGULAR STRUCTURE** — the line lengths and number of lines in each verse vary, creating a muddled, sleepy feel. Some lines are separated from the rest of the poem and there's virtually no punctuation.

Remember the Feelings and Attitudes in the Poem

1) The poet seems to have empathy for the man, e.g. the description of him "groggily" returning to reality (line 11).
2) There are fond memories of the Caribbean (lines 1-10).
3) There's also a subtle resentment at the London lifestyle and how it intrudes on his dreams (lines 16-18).
4) The poem concludes with a feeling of resignation and dread at the prospect of "Another London day".

Think About Your Feelings and Attitudes to the Poem

1) Pick 2 words or phrases that stand out to you. If none stand out, just pick 2 unusual words or phrases.
2) Write these 2 words or phrases down. Then write about how they make you feel. If they don't make you feel anything, don't worry — just make something up, as long as it's not too stupid.

> **EXAMPLE** The line "Another London day" at the end of the poem makes me feel sympathy for the man. To wake up after dreaming about paradise and then realise that you have to face another boring day must be really disheartening. The word "another" suggests he goes through this experience every day.

It's dreamy but it still has a serious point

'Island Man' deals with different cultures in a more nostalgic, easy-going way — it's certainly less cutting than 'Limbo' and 'Nothing's Changed'. But it still revolves around a clash of cultures and a feeling of isolation. Me, I still dream of the green, green fields of Stoke...

Imtiaz Dharker

Imtiaz Dharker was born in 1954 in Pakistan. She has said that she believes identity comes from "beliefs and states of mind", rather than nationality or religion.

Blessing

> The skin cracks like a pod.
> There never is enough water.
>
> Imagine the drip of it,
> the small splash, echo
> 5 in a tin mug,
> the voice of a kindly god.
>
> Sometimes, the sudden rush
> of fortune. The municipal pipe bursts,
> silver crashes to the ground
> 10 and the flow has found
> a roar of tongues. From the huts,
> a congregation: every man woman
> child for streets around
> butts in, with pots,
> 15 brass, copper, aluminium,
> plastic buckets,
> frantic hands,
>
> and naked children
> screaming in the liquid sun,
> 20 their highlights polished to perfection,
> flashing light,
> as the blessing sings
> over their small bones.

Annotations:
- "The skin cracks like a pod." — This could refer to the people's dry skin, or to cracks in dry ground.
- "There never is enough water." — This simple statement sets the scene for what follows.
- "Imagine" — It's been so long since they've had water, they have to imagine it, rather than remember it.
- "the small splash, echo / in a tin mug" — Even a tiny amount makes a big impact when there's so little around.
- "the voice of a kindly god." — Water is an answer to their prayers.
- "silver crashes to the ground" — This extended metaphor shows how valuable water is.
- "sudden rush / of fortune" — This phrase emphasises both the extent of the rush, and the commotion the water has caused.
- "a congregation" — This brings to mind a church — they worship the water.
- Short lines reflect the frantic rush for water.
- The irregular rhyme scheme adds to the bustling feel of the rush for water.
- Lack of punctuation creates a breathless effect.
- "liquid sun" — Emphasises the life-giving qualities of water.
- "highlights polished to perfection, / flashing light" — References to brightness and light create a religious feeling — a miracle has happened.
- "polished to perfection" — Alliteration makes this image really stand out.
- "as the blessing sings" — Another religious reference. What many people take for granted is seen here as something to be grateful for.
- "small bones" — Goes with the reference to skin in line 1, to create a sense of symmetry.

POEM DICTIONARY
municipal — to do with the city

Section One — The Poems

Blessing

Blessing is set in a massive slum called Dharavi, on the outskirts of Bombay. The poem describes the reactions of the people who live there to a burst water pipe, and how precious water is to them.

You've Got To Know What Happens in the Poem

Lines 1-6 — The poet describes the dryness of the slum, caused by drought and no water supply. We get a sense of how every drop of water is cherished by the people living in the slum.

Lines 7-17 — A water pipe bursts and loads of people frantically gather round to collect as much water as possible with anything that comes to hand (lines 14-16).

Lines 18-23 — The children of the slum are described, basking in the light of the "blessing" (line 22).

Learn About the Three Types of Language

1) **METAPHORICAL LANGUAGE** — the words used to describe water make it seem valuable. The people of the slum follow it like a religion (line 12).
2) **CHANGING TONE** — each verse has a feel of its own. The dreamy fantasy of water in verse 2 gives way to the frenzied pace of the rush when it appears for real. The final verse has a strange, religious feel.
3) **LIFE-RELATED LANGUAGE** — the reliance on water for survival is a constant theme.

Remember the Feelings and Attitudes in the Poem

1) There's a real desperation because of the lack of water — and the poet appeals to the reader to imagine how this would feel.
2) This desperation leads to the frantic urgency in collecting the water.
3) There's sheer delight at the rare pleasure of having water to drink. The poet uses the sight, sound and feel of water to give the reader an impression of the people's excitement.

Some water, yesterday

Think About Your Feelings and Attitudes to the Poem

1) Pick 2 words or phrases that stand out to you. If none stand out, just pick 2 unusual words or phrases.
2) Write these 2 words or phrases down. Then write about how they make you feel. If they don't make you feel anything, don't worry — just make something up, as long as it's not too stupid.

> **EXAMPLE** When I read the line "the sudden rush / of fortune", I have mixed feelings. The word "fortune" shows how valuable the water is, which makes me happy for the people of the slum, but it also shows how something that we take for granted seems like a miracle to them. It makes me feel grateful for what I've got.

This poem's not all it seems

It's an odd poem, this one. It's about people living in poverty and desperate to survive, but the tone seems to be quite upbeat — the people of the slum are ecstatic at the sight of water. But that also highlights just how poor they are. So even though it's short, there's lots to talk about in "Blessing".

Lawrence Ferlinghetti

Lawrence Ferlinghetti was born in New York in 1919. He settled in San Francisco and is interested in how different cultures and races mix. He's concerned about the growing gap between rich and poor.

Two Scavengers in a Truck, Two Beautiful People in a Mercedes

The title reflects the poem's contrasts — the lowly and disgusting scavengers versus the supposedly beautiful rich people.

The whole poem is about this short period of time.

At the stoplight waiting for the light
nine a.m. downtown San Francisco
a bright yellow garbage truck
with two garbagemen in red plastic blazers
5   standing on the back stoop
one on each side hanging on
and looking down into
an elegant open Mercedes
with an elegant couple in it
10   The man
in a hip three-piece linen suit
with shoulder-length blond hair & sunglasses
The young blond woman so casually coifed
with a short skirt and colored stockings
15   on the way to his architect's office

And the two scavengers up since four a.m.
grungy from their route
on the way home
The older of the two with grey iron hair
20   and hunched back
looking down like some
gargoyle Quasimodo
And the younger of the two
also with sunglasses & long hair
25   about the same age as the Mercedes driver

And both scavengers gazing down
as from a great distance
at the cool couple
as if they were watching some odorless TV ad
30   in which everything is always possible

And the very red light for an instant
holding all four close together
as if anything at all were possible
between them
35   across that small gulf
in the high seas
of this democracy

No movement.

Stark contrasts.

Repetition adds to the sarcastic tone of this word.

The contradiction suggests this image is false and hypocritical.

The lack of verbs adds to the feel of a still image — nothing is actually happening.

Something in common between the rich and poor.

Physically, they look down on the rich people, but only as ugly carved monsters might lurk over good people in church.

The observation is one-way — the rich couple don't pay the binmen any attention.

Another similarity, but only a superficial one.

This could have three meanings — fashionable, unfriendly, and cool in temperature, unlike the hot and sweaty binmen.

It's just a fantasy, and won't affect or touch them in any way.

It can't actually happen — it's just an illusion.

Emphasises that this won't last or change anything.

These two words contradict each other, emphasising that although the gap appears small, it's impossible to cross.

The layout leads to the stress on this last word, where the poet sarcastically refers to the idea of everyone having an equal say.

POEM DICTIONARY
stoop — rear footplate of a truck
coifed — stylishly arranged
Quasimodo — the fictional hunchbacked bell ringer of Notre Dame
hip — fashionable
gargoyle — a carved monster on the wall of a building
odorless — with no smell (American spelling)

Section One — The Poems

Two Scavengers in a Truck, Two Beautiful People in a Mercedes

This poem describes a frozen moment in time at a San Francisco traffic light. Two pairs of people from different backgrounds "meet". There's some strong social commentary about the gap between the rich and poor. Yeah, right on, fight the system! Anyway...

You've Got To Know What Happens in the Poem

Lines 1-9 — Two "garbagemen" (binmen to you and me) look down from their truck to see a rich, attractive couple in a flashy Mercedes car.

Lines 10-25 — The stark contrasts between the two pairs of people are described — the trendy clothes and expensive hair-dos of the couple in the Merc, and the dirty, tired binmen.

Lines 26-37 — The poet describes how far apart the pairs are in social terms, even though they're physically very close. This is dead important to the message of the poem.

Learn About the Three Types of Language

1) **STILLNESS** — the poem describes a single moment, and the odd layout spreads the phrases around like the different things you might notice in a photograph. There are no full stops — it's read in one go.

2) **COMPARISONS** — there are a few similarities between the rich and poor people, e.g. "sunglasses & long hair" (line 12), but there are also loads of differences.

3) **SOCIAL COMMENTARY** — this just means the poet says things about people and society. He often uses sarcasm to show his opinions, e.g. describing the rich people as "beautiful" and "elegant" (line 8), when he doesn't really admire them at all.

Remember the Feelings and Attitudes in the Poem

My social conscience must be in here somewhere...

1) The poet is fascinated with the extremes in society.
2) But he's also critical of society for allowing these extremes, and for making the differences between rich and poor so obvious.
3) There's a sense of the binmen longing for a life that they can't have and the rich couple being unaware or unconcerned by the contrast.

Think About Your Feelings and Attitudes to the Poem

1) Pick 2 words or phrases that stand out to you. If none stand out, just pick 2 unusual words or phrases.
2) Write these 2 words or phrases down. Then write about how they make you feel. If they don't make you feel anything, don't worry — just make something up, as long as it's not too stupid.

> **EXAMPLE** When the poet refers to the binmen as "scavengers", it makes me feel disgusted, but also sorry for them — they are forced to live off the scraps of hope offered by seeing how rich people live, and this feels very unfair.

It's set in the good ole US of A — but that's ok...

Ok, so there are words like "downtown", and "coloured" is spelt wrong, which makes it sound a bit yankee-doodle. But the themes and issues in the poem could apply just as much to our lovely old U of K — just substitute San Francisco for Bristol and you get the idea.

Section One — The Poems

Nissim Ezekiel

Nissim Ezekiel was born in Bombay in 1924, to Jewish parents. But he was raised in a mainly Hindu culture, and has been influenced by atheist views.

Night of the Scorpion

I remember the night my mother
was stung by a scorpion. Ten hours
of steady rain had driven him
to crawl beneath a sack of rice.
5 Parting with his poison – flash
of diabolic tail in the dark room –
he risked the rain again.
The peasants came like swarms of flies
and buzzed the name of God a hundred times
10 to paralyse the Evil One.
With candles and with lanterns
throwing giant scorpion shadows
on the mud-baked walls
they searched for him: he was not found.
15 They clicked their tongues.
With every movement that the scorpion made
his poison moved in Mother's blood, they said.
May he sit still, they said.
May the sins of your previous birth
20 be burned away tonight, they said.
May your suffering decrease
the misfortunes of your next birth, they said.
May the sum of evil
balanced in this unreal world
25 against the sum of good
become diminished by your pain.
May the poison purify your flesh
of desire, and your spirit of ambition,
they said, and they sat around
30 on the floor with my mother in the centre,
the peace of understanding on each face.
More candles, more lanterns, more neighbours,
more insects, and the endless rain.
My mother twisted through and through,
35 groaning on a mat.
My father, sceptic, rationalist,
trying every curse and blessing,
powder, mixture, herb and hybrid.
He even poured a little paraffin
40 upon the bitten toe and put a match to it.
I watched the flame feeding on my mother.
I watched the holy man perform his rites
to tame the poison with an incantation.
After twenty hours
45 it lost its sting.

My mother only said
Thank God the scorpion picked on me
and spared my children.

Annotations:
- It's from the child's point of view. But he's an outsider throughout — he can't affect anything.
- He uses a straightforward tone to describe the incident.
- These words set the scene by showing it's a poor Indian home.
- The scorpion is seen as symbolic of the devil.
- This simile makes the villagers seem panic-stricken and illogical.
- Again, this shows it's a poor Indian home.
- A terrifying image, especially for a child.
- They don't seem very bothered about failing to find the scorpion.
- The villagers are talking about her reincarnation — they think she'll die.
- Sounds like a prayer. But having the same word at the start of so many lines makes this reaction seem repetitive and unthinking. "They said" is also repeated at the end of many lines.
- Pain is seen as a way of cleansing the soul before the next life.
- There's an ironic feel to this — their reaction has been far from understanding or peaceful.
- This shocking sight clearly lives on in the poet's memory, even as an adult.
- This shows how desperate the situation is.
- All he can do is watch. The holy man's actions seem baffling to him.
- There's a ceremonial feel to the holy man's actions — they don't seem like a practical solution.
- The matter-of-fact tone suggests this was the inevitable outcome — the panic was unnecessary.
- He admires his mother for staying calm after all she's been through, and through everyone else's panic.

POEM DICTIONARY
diabolic — to do with the devil
diminished — reduced
sceptic — a doubtful person
rationalist — a person who uses logical thinking to explain things
hybrid — a mixture of things
rites — actions in a ceremony
incantation — religious chanting

Section One — The Poems

Night of the Scorpion

The poet remembers a time when he was a child when his mother was stung by a scorpion. He describes the reactions of various religious people — and seems to think they're all a bit silly. In the end, his mum survives anyway. I love a happy ending...

You've Got To Know What Happens in the Poem

Lines 1-7   The poet remembers how a scorpion, which had come inside to escape the rain, stung his mum.

Lines 8-33   Some locals come round and look for the scorpion, but they can't find the blighter (line 14). They try to help the woman, saying religious stuff about reincarnation — they clearly think his mum's going to die.

Lines 34-48   His mum's in agony (lines 34-35). His dad does everything he can to cure her. Then, after all the fuss, she pulls through, and just thanks God it was her and not her children (lines 47-48).

Learn About the Three Types of Language

1) **FACTUAL TONE** — there's a neutral, straightforward way of talking when the poet describes the more action-based parts of the story, e.g. the stinging incident (lines 1-4). This contrasts with the more ceremonial feel of the religious language.

2) **THE CHILD'S PERSPECTIVE** — it's a first person narrative, so we witness the events through the child's eyes. He's confused and frightened, as any child would be.

3) **RELIGIOUS LANGUAGE** — it's set in a Hindu community, where they believe in reincarnation — so there's lots of stuff about purifying the soul of sin for the next life (lines 19-28).

Remember the Feelings and Attitudes in the Poem

1) The poet is frightened by what's happening, but admires his mum's courage.
2) There's a sense of panic in the villagers' reactions. Even his dad, who isn't religious, goes along with the religious stuff (lines 36-40).
3) The poet seems critical of religion — the ceremonial language and all that talk of the next life seem unhelpful and premature.

Think About Your Feelings and Attitudes to the Poem

1) Pick 2 words or phrases that stand out to you. If none stand out, just pick 2 unusual words or phrases.
2) Write these 2 words or phrases down. Then write about how they make you feel. If they don't make you feel anything, don't worry — just make something up, as long as it's not too stupid.

> **EXAMPLE**   The phrase "the flame feeding on my mother" makes me feel very uneasy, as it sounds like she's being eaten alive. It seems to me that these 'cures' are actually making his mother's suffering worse, rather than reducing it.

Compare the last bit to the rest of the poem

The final three lines of the poem are separated from the rest. This last bit's about the mother's calm, unselfish reaction. It's separate because it's a clear contrast to the panic of the rest of the poem. After all, it's only a scorpion, it's not like it's poisonous or summat... Eh? Oh, right.

Section One — The Poems

Chinua Achebe

> ... Thus the Commandant at Belsen
> Camp going home for
> the day with fumes of
> human roast clinging
> rebelliously to his hairy
> nostrils will stop
> at the wayside sweet-shop
> and pick up a chocolate
> for his tender offspring
> waiting at home for Daddy's
> return...
>   Praise bounteous
> providence if you will
> that grants even an ogre
> a tiny glow-worm
> tenderness encapsulated
> in icy caverns of a cruel
> heart or else despair
> for in the very germ
> of that kindred love is
> lodged the perpetuity
> of evil.

(lines 30–50)

Annotations:
- This bit links the first section about the vultures to the second section about the Commandant.
- Evil is personified too, as a persistent reminder of what the Commandant has been doing.
- The Commandant is physically unattractive, like the vultures.
- Says he's not sure how to look at it — he invites the reader to decide.
- The poem concludes on a dark note.
- Makes it sound like he's a normal person with a normal job.
- The children are described as if they're meat — linking them to the "human roast".
- He has a different name when connected with his family — like it's a different version of himself.
- Sounds inhuman — like a monster.
- Contrasts of size and lightness.
- The poet seems to think evil will never go away — it's part of human nature.

POEM DICTIONARY
harbinger — a messenger / a sign of things to come
charnel-house — a place where corpses are stored
Commandant — a commanding officer
Belsen — a Nazi concentration camp, where people (mostly Jews) were held and killed during World War II
bounteous providence — the good things that God has given to mankind
encapsulated — enclosed
perpetuity — lasting forever

Section One — The Poems

Chinua Achebe

Chinua Achebe was born in Nigeria in 1931. He worked for the Nigerian Broadcasting Corporation, but when war broke out in 1967, he started to work for the government of Biafra (an area that violently split from the rest of Nigeria). He's written lots of poems about war and its effects.

Vultures

All these words are related to darkness and misery. They set the tone of the poem.

In the greyness
and drizzle of one despondent
dawn unstirred by harbingers
of sunbreak a vulture
5 perching high on broken
bone of a dead tree
nestled close to his
mate his smooth
bashed-in head, a pebble
10 on a stem rooted in
a dump of gross
feathers, inclined affectionately
to hers. Yesterday they picked
the eyes of a swollen
15 corpse in a water-logged
trench and ate the
things in its bowel. Full
gorged they chose their roost
keeping the hollowed remnant
20 in easy range of cold
telescopic eyes ...
    Strange
indeed how love in other
ways so particular
25 will pick a corner
in that charnel-house
tidy it and coil up there, perhaps
even fall asleep – her face
turned to the wall!

The vulture's ugliness adds to the evil mood.

Nothing is too disgusting for the vultures.

Having this word on its own sounds like he's stopping to ponder on it.

Love ignores evil, instead of triumphing over it — they exist separately.

The vultures live off death.

This phrase stands out against the ugliness of the vulture.

Violent image suggests the horror of war.

They see it as an object rather than something that has been alive.

Personification of love.

The idea of love sleeping among corpses is a very bleak image.

Section One — The Poems

THIS IS A FLAP.
FOLD THIS PAGE OUT.

Vultures

This poem's pretty grim. We're told how a pair of vultures, despite having some <u>disgusting</u> eating habits, are still capable of <u>affection</u> for each other. The poet compares the vultures to a <u>Nazi officer</u> who's <u>cruel and murderous</u> during the day but <u>loving and kind</u> when he's with his family.

You've Got To Know What Happens in the Poem

<u>Lines 1-21</u>   A pair of <u>vultures</u> are described, scoffing down <u>eyes</u> and stuff. Nice.

<u>Lines 22-29</u> The poet discusses how <u>odd</u> it is that love — seen here as a <u>person</u> — chooses to <u>ignore</u> the presence of evil.

<u>Lines 30-40</u> A <u>Nazi commandant</u> goes home, with the smell of <u>murder</u> clinging to him (lines 32-35). He buys some <u>sweets</u> for his child waiting for him at home (lines 37-38).

<u>Lines 41-51</u> The poet finishes by saying you could look at it <u>two ways</u>: on the one hand you could be <u>grateful</u> that such an <u>evil</u> person even has a <u>shred of decency</u> in him (lines 41-47)... on the other hand, the good inside that person will always be <u>infected with evil</u> (lines 47-51).

Learn About the Three Types of Language

1) **CONTEMPLATIVE TONE** — although the poet talks about disgusting things, he <u>doesn't say outright</u> that he's appalled by them. He <u>contemplates</u> the evil that humans are capable of, and how love can't seem to conquer cruelty — he says it's "strange" (line 22), rather than tragic.

2) **EVIL MOOD** — the poem starts at dawn, but there's <u>no sign of the sun</u> (lines 3-4). There are loads of words related to <u>darkness</u>, <u>death</u> and <u>ugliness</u> — a sombre mood hangs over the poem.

3) **METAPHORICAL LANGUAGE** — the <u>vultures</u> are a metaphor for evil behaviour of people. There's a lot of <u>symbolism</u> — love is seen as a <u>person</u>, who chooses not to notice the less pleasant aspects of humanity (lines 22-29).

Remember the Feelings and Attitudes in the Poem

Who's a pretty boy then?

1) The poet finds the appearance and behaviour of the vultures (lines 8-21) and the Commandant (30-35) <u>unpleasant</u>.

2) But he's <u>not shocked</u> by it. His disgust is detached and <u>unemotional</u> — although this apparent lack of surprise may be intended to <u>shock the reader</u>.

3) He's <u>unsure</u> about how to look at the fact that people are capable of both kindness and cruelty (41-51).

Think About Your Feelings and Attitudes to the Poem

1) Pick 2 words or phrases that <u>stand out to you</u>. If none stand out, just pick 2 <u>unusual words or phrases</u>.

2) Write these 2 words or phrases down. Then write about how they <u>make you feel</u>. If they don't make you feel anything, don't worry — just <u>make something up</u>, as long as it's <u>not too stupid</u>.

> **EXAMPLE** The phrase "a tiny glow-worm / of tenderness" makes me feel very depressed. Although good exists in the Commandant, it seems so insignificant when compared to the "icy caverns" of cruelty — it seems impossible that goodness will come out on top.

The link between the vultures and the man is crucial

The stuff about vultures, even though there's a lot of it, is there mainly as a way of <u>introducing</u> the topic of good and evil in <u>people</u>, or as a metaphor for the Nazi Commandant. It's as if the poet's seen the vultures feeding, and it's <u>reminded</u> him of the fact that people can do dreadful things.

Section One — The Poems

Denise Levertov

Denise Levertov (1923-97) was born in England but moved to New York in 1947. She later became an American citizen, but was strongly opposed to the USA's involvement in the Vietnam War.

What Were They Like?

1) Did the people of Viet Nam
   use lanterns of stone?
2) Did they hold ceremonies
   to reverence the opening of buds?
3) Were they inclined to quiet laughter?
4) Did they use bone and ivory,
   jade and silver, for ornament?
5) Had they an epic poem?
6) Did they distinguish between speech and singing?

1) Sir, their light hearts turned to stone.
   It is not remembered whether in gardens
   stone lanterns illumined pleasant ways.
2) Perhaps they gathered once to delight in blossom,
   but after the children were killed
   there were no more buds)
3) Sir, laughter is bitter to the burned mouth.
4) A dream ago, perhaps. Ornament is for joy.
   All the bones were charred.
5) It is not remembered. Remember,
   most were peasants; their life
   was in rice and bamboo.
   When peaceful clouds were reflected in the paddies
   and the water buffalo stepped surely along terraces,
   maybe fathers told their sons old tales.
   When bombs smashed those mirrors
   there was time only to scream.
6) There is an echo yet
   of their speech which was like a song.
   It was reported that their singing resembled
   the flight of moths in moonlight.
   Who can say? It is silent now.

© 'What Were They Like?' from Selected Poems (Bloodaxe Books, 1986). Reproduced by permission of Pollinger Limited and the proprietor.

POEM DICTIONARY
reverence — deep respect or worship
illumined — lit up
paddies — waterlogged fields for growing rice
jade — a gemstone, normally green
charred — blackened by fire
terraces — different levels of fields for farming

Section One — The Poems

What Were They Like?

This poem is written as though Vietnamese culture is a thing of the past and someone is trying to find out about it. They ask six questions but the answers reveal that the devastation caused by the war has removed all traces of the culture.

You've Got To Know What Happens in the Poem

Verse 1 — This is a series of questions about how Vietnamese people used to live before the war. It asks about their way of life (Questions 1 and 4), their culture (Q2 and Q5), their behaviour (Q3), and their language (Q6).

Verse 2 — This answers the questions one by one. We're told that they used to be light-hearted and happy, but the war changed that (Answer 1 and 3). Their history is lost and their culture destroyed. The tone of the answers is vague and uncertain, as if the person speaking them can't be sure about life before the war (Answer 6).

Learn About the Four Types of Language

1) **RESPECTFUL LANGUAGE** — the poet sees the Vietnamese people and culture as beautiful and admirable (e.g. Answer 5). This makes the destruction caused by the war seem even more appalling.

2) **METAPHORICAL LANGUAGE** — there's a mythical feel to some of the language (e.g. Answer 5). This is related to the old stories and ceremonies of the Vietnamese culture.

> There's often a mix of formal and metaphorical language in the same sentence, e.g. Answer 1. This suggests the person replying might be reporting back on rumours they've heard.

3) **FORMAL TONE** — it's based around the style of a formal military investigation. Answers 1 and 3 start with "Sir" — like a soldier reporting back to his superior officer.

4) **SENSE OF DEVASTATION** — war and destruction are constant themes. The whole poem is in the past tense, suggesting that everything that's being described has been lost for ever.

Remember the Feelings and Attitudes in the Poem

A paddy field

1) On the surface of it, the tone is formal and unemotional (e.g. Question 1).
2) But really the poet is sad at what has happened, and angry at those responsible (Answers 3 and 4). She criticises the thoughtlessness of the war.
3) There's a sense of regret at what has been lost (Answer 6).

Think About Your Feelings and Attitudes to the Poem

1) Pick 2 words or phrases that stand out to you. If none stand out, just pick 2 unusual words or phrases.
2) Write these 2 words or phrases down. Then write about how they make you feel. If they don't make you feel anything, don't worry — just make something up, as long as it's not too stupid.

> **EXAMPLE** The phrase, "It is silent now", at the end of the poem, makes me feel desperately sad, because it seems that the war has completely destroyed this beautiful culture.

Match each answer to its question

You might find it useful to tackle the poem by reading one question, then the matching answer — this way, you can see how the use of one word changes between the question and the answer, e.g. "stone" in Q1 and A1. Also, reading up on the background to the Vietnam War will help loads.

Section One — The Poems

Sujata Bhatt

Sujata Bhatt was born in India in 1956, later lived in the USA and now lives in Germany. She writes in both English and Gujarati, her mother tongue.

from Search For My Tongue

> You ask me what I mean
> by saying I have lost my tongue.
> I ask you, what would you do
> if you had two tongues in your mouth,
> 5   and lost the first one, the mother tongue,
> and could not really know the other,
> the foreign tongue.
> You could not use them both together
> even if you thought that way.
> 10 And if you lived in a place you had to
> speak a foreign tongue,
> your mother tongue would rot,
> rot and die in your mouth
> until you had to spit it out.
> 15 I thought I spit it out
> but overnight while I dream,
>
> મને હતું કે આખી જીભ આખી ભાષા.
> (munay hutoo kay aakhee jeebh aakhee bhasha)
> મેં થૂંકી નાખી છે.
> 20 (may thoonky nakhi chay)
> પરંતુ રાત્રે સ્વપ્નમાં મારી ભાષા પાછી આવે છે.
> (parantoo rattray svupnama mari bhasha pachi aavay chay)
> ફૂલની જેમ મારી ભાષા મારી જીભ
> (foolnee jaim mari bhasha mari jeebh)
> 25 મોઢામાં ખીલે છે.
> (modhama kheelay chay)
> ફૂલની જેમ મારી ભાષા મારી જીભ
> (fullnee jaim mari bhasha mari jeebh)
> મોઢામાં પાકે છે.
> 30 (modhama pakay chay)
> it grows back, a stump of a shoot
> grows longer, grows moist, grows strong veins,
> it ties the other tongue in knots,
> the bud opens, the bud opens in my mouth,
> 35 it pushes the other tongue aside.
> Everytime I think I've forgotten,
> I think I've lost the mother tongue,
> it blossoms out of my mouth.

Annotations:
- She uses 'I' and 'you' a lot, like in a conversation.
- Double meaning of "couldn't speak", and "lost my language".
- Uses image of two tongues in a mouth to represent speaking two languages.
- Gets 'you' to imagine what her situation is like. This gets the reader involved.
- These words are emphasised by being on a separate line.
- Conflict.
- Repetition strengthens the horrible image.
- Unpleasant image.
- Repetition makes the image stronger.
- The Gujarati language is spelt out phonetically in English so we can read it and hear the sounds.
- Visual contrast to the rest of the poem.
- A metaphor is used in this part of the poem. The mother tongue is described as if it's a growing plant.
- She's still using the image of two tongues competing inside her mouth.
- The repetition of 'grows' and the word 'strong' make the mother tongue sound healthy and robust.
- Repeated — for a feeling of wonder and suspense.
- She makes the mother tongue sound like a part of nature, with a life and strength of its own.
- The plant metaphor is completed with the image of the plant bursting into flower.

POEM DICTIONARY
mother tongue — a person's first language

Section One — The Poems

Search For My Tongue

This poem is about the <u>conflict</u> between the poet's first language and the foreign language she now uses. The poet is really <u>worried</u> she'll <u>forget her first language</u> (mother tongue), but it turns out all right in the end — her mother tongue is always with her in her dreams. Ahhhhh...

You've Got To Know the Structure of the Poem

<u>Lines 1-15</u>   Explains the <u>problem</u> she has of being <u>fluent in two languages</u>. She uses the image of having "two tongues in your mouth" to explain what it is like.

<u>Lines 16-30</u>   When she's asleep she <u>dreams in her mother tongue</u>. This is in the middle of the poem because it's at the centre of the conflict she is experiencing.

<u>Lines 31-38</u>   Describes how her <u>mother tongue grows back</u> every time she thinks she has forgotten it — it is stronger and "pushes the other tongue aside" (line 35).

Learn About the Three Types of Language

1) **CONVERSATIONAL LANGUAGE** — in the first part of the poem, the poet uses chatty language (e.g. "I ask you", line 3). It makes it sound like she's <u>talking to the reader</u> about her problem.

2) **FOREIGN LANGUAGE** — in the middle part of the poem, there is <u>Gujarati</u> language. This shows us her mother tongue visually, and emphasises its difference from English.

3) **METAPHORICAL LANGUAGE** — In the last part of the poem she uses more poetic language — very different from the chatty language in the first part of the poem. She uses the metaphor of her mother tongue growing back like a flower.

> **DOUBLE MEANING**
> "Tongue" can mean both the fleshy thing in your mouth and a language.

Remember the Feelings and Attitudes in the Poem

1) She <u>worries</u> that she is <u>forgetting her mother tongue</u> — and that her second language will never feel as natural (lines 1-7).

2) This is part of a bigger worry that she might <u>lose her Indian identity</u> by living in another country. She's concerned that she's <u>stuck between different cultures</u> (lines 4-9).

3) She's <u>happy</u> when she realises that her mother tongue will <u>always be a part of her</u> — "it <u>blossoms</u> out of my mouth."

4) She could be challenging the way English has <u>taken over</u> in many parts of the world, resulting in other languages <u>dying out</u>.

Think About Your Feelings and Attitudes to the Poem

1) Pick 2 words or phrases that <u>stand out to you</u>. If none stand out, just pick 2 <u>unusual words or phrases</u>.

2) Write these 2 words or phrases down. Then write about how they <u>make you feel</u>. If they don't make you feel anything, don't worry — just <u>make something up</u>, as long as it's not too stupid.

> **EXAMPLE**   On line 38, the poet describes how her mother tongue "blossoms out" of her mouth. I feel this is a particularly powerful image, as it suggests the force of nature is with her when she speaks Gujarati.

This poem is about more than languages...

This poem highlights the difficulties of being part of two cultures — <u>language</u> is an essential part of <u>culture and identity</u>. There's more about identity on page 34 — other poets focus on this topic too.

Section One — The Poems

Tom Leonard

Tom Leonard was born in Glasgow in 1944. He's often written about people's attitudes to different accents, and says he writes in Scottish dialect so that his 'voice' can be heard through his poetry.

from Unrelated Incidents

this is thi
six a clock
news thi
man said n
5 thi reason
a talk wia
BBC accent
iz coz yi
widny wahnt
10 mi ti talk
aboot thi
trooth wia
voice lik
wanna yoo
15 scruff. if
a toktaboot
thi trooth
lik wanna yoo
scruff yi
20 widny thingk
it wuz troo.
jist wanna yoo
scruff tokn.
thirza right
25 way ti spell
ana right way
ti tok it. this
is me tokn yir
right way a
30 spellin. this
is ma trooth
yooz doant no
thi trooth
yirsellz cawz
35 yi canny talk
right. this is
the six a clock
nyooz. belt up.

Annotations

- The lack of capital letters and speech marks makes it sound informal — like someone's talking. This also shows that the poet won't be forced into using standard English.
- Cliché of a posh English accent.
- "with a"
- "wouldn't want"
- The short lines make the poem look like a newsreader's autocue, scrolling quickly down for easy reading. They also add to the abrupt, no-nonsense feel of the dialect.
- "commoners"
- "talked about"
- Says that even people with regional accents don't want to hear the news read in one.
- Sounds very disrespectful towards working-class people.
- Clearly the newsreader sees regional accents as "the wrong way".
- There's an irony in the supposed mis-spelling of "spelling".
- Suggests there are different versions of the truth according to what background you're from.
- "you can't"
- This defiant way of announcing the news comes across as slightly comical here.
- He imitates the newsreader's posh accent in this last bit.
- Working-class people are denied the chance to have their voices heard on the news.

Section One — The Poems

Unrelated Incidents

This poem's about people's attitudes towards <u>accents</u>. The poet imagines a newsreader saying that the news has got to be read in a <u>posh accent</u>, because if it was read in a working-class, regional accent, no one would take it seriously. Confusingly, all this is described in <u>Scottish dialect</u>.

You've Got To Know What Happens in the Poem

Lines 1-15	The poet *imagines* a newsreader saying to him, "I talk with a posh accent because no one wants to hear the news read in a common accent like yours."
Lines 15-23	"If I talked like you, you wouldn't think it was true — you'd think it was just one of you commoners talking."
Lines 24-30	"There's a right way to spell and talk. I'm talking the right way."
Lines 30-38	"This is my truth. You don't know the truth because you can't talk right. Shut up."

Learn About the Two Types of Language

1) **SCOTTISH ACCENT and DIALECT** — the words are spelt phonetically, i.e. they're spelt like they sound. This is vital to the ironic effect of hearing someone with a strong regional accent mocking someone who doesn't like accents.

2) **POLITICAL LANGUAGE** — accents are linked to class. The poet says that working-class people are denied the chance to use their own voice (lines 32-38). When they listen to the news, it's a posh English person telling them the "trooth".

> **ACCENT AND DIALECT**
>
> *Accent* means the way people pronounce certain words.
> *Dialect* means the words and grammar a person uses, and their accent.

Not all Scottish people look like this.

Remember the Feelings and Attitudes in the Poem

1) He's annoyed at the dominance of posh, English accents in the media, and about how working-class, regional accents are not heard.
2) He mocks the idea of snobby people looking down on regional accents as inferior (lines 35-36).
3) He criticises this snobbery in a sarcastic way, by "translating" it into his own dialect.
4) What he's getting at overall is that you shouldn't judge people by the way they talk.

Think About Your Feelings and Attitudes to the Poem

1) Pick 2 words or phrases that stand out to you. If none stand out, just pick 2 unusual words or phrases.
2) Write these 2 words or phrases down. Then write about how they make you feel. If they don't make you feel anything, don't worry — just make something up, as long as it's not too stupid.

> **EXAMPLE** The phrase "wanna yoo scruff" makes me annoyed at the arrogance of the newsreader. He seems to look down on people with regional accents just because of the way they talk.

Think about how the poem sounds when it's spoken

Almost the whole poem's written in <u>dialect</u>, which can make it a tad <u>tricky to understand</u> if you're not used to it. Try to 'hear' it in your head — or even read it out loud — then imagine the bloke out of <u>Taggart</u> saying it. An uf thaht disnae help, muv tae Scoatland fer a bit, ye moanin Sassenach.

Section One — The Poems

John Agard

> Explain yuself
> wha yu mean
> Ah listening to yu wid de keen
> half of mih ear
> 35 Ah lookin at yu wid de keen
> half of mih eye
> and when I'm introduced to yu
> I'm sure you'll understand
> why I offer yu half-a-hand
> 40 an when I sleep at night
> I close half-a-eye
> consequently when I dream
> I dream half-a-dream
> an when moon begin to glow
> 45 I half-caste human being
> cast half-a-shadow
> but yu must come back tomorrow
> wid de whole of yu eye
> an de whole of yu ear
> 50 an de whole of yu mind
>
> an I will tell yu
> de other half
> of my story

Annotations:
- Shows he's willing to hear other points of view.
- He's scrutinising you.
- He extends the idea of being "half" to the individual parts of his body, to show how silly it is.
- Suggests people have made their minds up without even meeting him.
- Nonsensical images show how silly the idea of being half of something is.
- People have to change their attitudes.
- Rhyming makes it seem like a well-planned argument, rather than a rant.
- Implies people only see what they want to see.
- Suggests the person he's talking to is narrow-minded.
- Takes the idea to its extreme — that the poem itself is only half the story.

POEM DICTIONARY
Picasso — the name of a 20th Century Spanish painter
Tchaikovsky — the name of a 19th Century Russian classical music composer

Section One — The Poems

John Agard

John Agard was born in Guyana in South America in 1949, to parents of mixed nationality. He came to Britain in 1977. He likes to perform his poems, and believes humour is an effective way of challenging people's opinions.

Half-Caste

Excuse me
standing on one leg
I'm half-caste

[Introduces the subject in a jokey way, poking fun at the term "half-caste".]

Explain yuself
5 wha yu mean
when yu say half-caste
yu mean when picasso
mix red an green
is a half-caste canvas/
10 explain yuself
wha yu mean
when yu say half-caste
yu mean when light an shadow
mix in de sky
15 is a half-caste weather/
well in dat case
england weather
nearly always half-caste
in fact some o dem cloud
20 half-caste till dem overcast
so spiteful dem dont want de sun pass
ah rass/
explain yuself
wha yu mean
25 when yu say half-caste
yu mean tchaikovsky
sit down at dah piano
an mix a black key
wid a white key
30 is a half-caste symphony/

Annotations:
- Conversational but aggressive tone — this is repeated several times.
- He compares having parents of different colour to mixing the colours of a great painting.
- He uses a chatty tone, like he's reasoning with someone in an argument.
- His use of creole, mixed in with standard English, shows he's comfortable with the different sides to his background.
- Expression of disgust.
- He says we wouldn't have had great music without mixing colours together.
- Lack of capital letters could suggest everyone's equal (also on lines 17 and 26).
- Natural image — shows there's nothing wrong with colours mixing.
- Plays with the double meaning of cast/caste.
- Piano music uses a mixture of black and white keys, but people don't call it half-caste — so why are people who are part black and part white described like that?

Section One — The Poems

THIS IS A FLAP.
FOLD THIS PAGE OUT.

Half-Caste

The poet makes fun of the term "half-caste" (someone with parents of different colour). He sees himself as being a _mix_ of things — rather than _half_ of something — and compares it to loads of other things which are great because they're made up of mixtures, like _paintings_ and _symphonies_.

You've Got To Know What Happens in the Poem

Lines 1-30 — The poet asks what the term "half-caste" is supposed to _mean_. He says if you look at things like that, then everything that's _mixed_ could be called half-caste, like great _paintings_ (lines 6-9), the _weather_ (13-15), and _classical music_ (26-30).

Lines 31-53 — He _challenges_ people to explain their way of thinking, but finds no logic in it.
He _mocks_ the idea by talking about "halves" of other things, e.g. line 34.
He says people should _sort their ideas out_, by opening their eyes and their minds.

Learn About the Three Types of Language

1) **METAPHORICAL LANGUAGE** — he compares being of mixed race to the different colours of a _painting_, showing it's _beautiful_, and to the _weather_, showing it's _natural_. This is central to his argument against the term "half-caste", which he sees as _negative_ and _very insulting_.

2) **HUMOUR** — he makes the idea of being "half" of something _laughable_. His humour isn't always light-hearted — his jokes about being half a person are quite _scathing_ (e.g. line 39).

3) **ARGUMENTATIVE TONE** — the style is _conversational_ — "yu" and "I" are used a lot — but also _confrontational_. He challenges assumptions by repeatedly saying "Explain yuself" (lines 4, 10, 23, 31). He uses Caribbean _creole_ (dialect) and _no punctuation_, which makes it sound direct and informal.

Remember the Feelings and Attitudes in the Poem

1) He _mocks_ the idea of mixed-race people being inferior or "incomplete".
2) He's _baffled_ and _amused_ by the idea of being half a person.
3) He gets _angry_ that people aren't more open-minded, and he _tells off_ these people at the end (lines 47-50).

Half a horse

Think About Your Feelings and Attitudes to the Poem

1) Pick 2 words or phrases that _stand out to you_. If none stand out, just pick 2 _unusual words or phrases_.
2) Write these 2 words or phrases down. Then write about how they _make you feel_. If they don't make you feel anything, don't worry — just _make something up_, as long as it's _not too stupid_.

> **EXAMPLE** The phrase "half-a-hand" seems funny and absurd. It's a bizarre image, and just shows how ridiculous it is to use the word "half-caste" to describe a person.

The jokes are crucial to the point being made

A good way to pick up marks here is to talk about _how_ the humour helps the poet _make his point_. It's not good enough just to say a line's funny — you have to _interpret_ what he's actually getting at.

Section One — The Poems

Derek Walcott

Derek Walcott was born in St Lucia, in the West Indies, in 1930.
His father was English and his mother was African.
As well as poetry, he's written plays, and is a painter.

Love After Love

The time will come
When, with elation,
You will greet yourself arriving
At your own door, in your own mirror,
5   And each will smile at the other's welcome,

And say sit here. Eat.
You will love again the stranger who was your self.
Give wine. Give bread. Give back your heart
To itself, to the stranger who has loved you

10 All your life, whom you ignored
For another, who knows you by heart.
Take down the love-letters from the bookshelf

The photographs, the desperate notes,
Peel your own images from the mirror.
15 Sit. Feast on your life.

Annotations:

- Positive prediction.
- There's a formal acknowledgement of this "meeting".
- The repetition of the word 'will' sounds confident and assured.
- Makes the idea of greeting yourself a visual image.
- Suggests returning to something or someone you abandoned.
- Short sentences are used for calm, simple instructions.
- Christian connection — suggests this is a spiritual process.
- The self is seen as an abused lover who has remained loyal.
- Suggests that loving another person can be a betrayal of the self.
- This continues the sentence that starts on line 8.
- Another person could never know you as deeply as your self does.
- The poet encourages the reader to put the past behind them and move on.
- Suggests removing the false outer layers to reveal the true, inner self.
- Links the theme of eating to the idea that there's loads to celebrate and look forward to.
- The only negativity in the poem comes from references to relationships with other people.

Section One — The Poems

Love After Love

"Love After Love" is about finding <u>happiness</u> on your own after the end of a relationship. The poet says that being in love can make you forget who you <u>really are</u>. So beautiful (sniff)...

You've Got To Know What Happens in the Poem

Lines 1-5	The poet says confidently that, after splitting up with someone, you'll eventually return to your <u>own identity</u> (lines 3-5) — and you'll be <u>happy</u> about it ("with elation", line 2).
Lines 6-11	There are offerings of <u>food and drink</u> (line 8) — it's a <u>celebration</u>. He says you should get to know your "self" again, as you know yourself better than any other person (line 11).
Lines 12-15	He suggests <u>removing</u> all the signs of previous relationships, like <u>photos</u> and stuff (12-13). Just chill out and <u>make the most</u> of your life (line 15).

Learn About the Three Types of Language

1) **CEREMONIAL LANGUAGE** — there are <u>religious</u> references (line 8), and a formal-sounding <u>greeting</u> (line 3). At times it sounds like a religious rite of passage (lines 8 and 15), marking a <u>new start in life</u>.

2) **REFERENCES TO THE "SELF"** — the "self" is seen as more than just an identity — it's a person <u>within you</u>. The message of the poem is that you <u>neglect</u> this self when you love another person ("whom you ignored", line 10), so you should <u>get to know it</u> again.

3) **INSTRUCTIVE LANGUAGE** — the style is like a <u>self-help</u> book. It's <u>advice</u> that the poet wants to pass down. There's no "maybe" or "possibly" about it — these things <u>will</u> happen (e.g. line 1).

Remember the Feelings and Attitudes in the Poem

Cheers. Here's to me.

1) He's <u>positive</u> and <u>optimistic</u>. He says it's good to have time to get to know yourself again. He thinks you'll be <u>better off</u> this way than you would be living with someone else.

2) There's a <u>calm assurance</u> about the poem. He's <u>reflecting</u> on his own experiences over a long period of time, and he seems <u>confident</u> that what he's saying is good advice.

Think About Your Feelings and Attitudes to the Poem

1) Pick 2 words or phrases that <u>stand out to you</u>. If none stand out, just pick 2 <u>unusual words or phrases</u>.
2) Write these 2 words or phrases down. Then write about how they <u>make you feel</u>. If they don't make you feel anything, don't worry — just <u>make something up</u>, as long as it's <u>not too stupid</u>.

It's OK to be critical like this sometimes — as long as you make sure you explain why you don't like it.

EXAMPLE I'm annoyed by the phrase "Give back your heart / To itself". Just because he prefers to be single, he tries to discourage other people from finding happiness with someone else. This attitude seems selfish and defeatist to me.

Exam After Exam

The day will come when, with reluctance, you must face an exam. You will greet your teacher, arriving in the Sports Hall. And he will say, "Sit here. Write your name on the front of the paper. Take pens. Take pencils. Give back all revision materials. Sit. Feast on your exam."

Section One — The Poems

Imtiaz Dharker

Imtiaz Dharker was born in 1954 in Pakistan. She has said that she believes identity comes from "beliefs and states of mind", rather than nationality or religion.

This Room

This room is breaking out
of itself, cracking through
its own walls
in search of space, light,
5   empty air.

The bed is lifting out of
its nightmares.
From dark corners, chairs
are rising up to crash through clouds.

10 This is the time and place
to be alive:
when the daily furniture of our lives
stirs, when the improbable arrives.
Pots and pans bang together
15 in celebration, clang
past the crowd of garlic, onions, spices,
fly by the ceiling fan.
No one is looking for the door.

In all this excitement
20 I'm wondering where
I've left my feet, and why

my hands are outside, clapping.

Annotations:
- Personification of the room.
- An almost miraculous image.
- Positive, upward movement.
- Everyday surroundings seem to come to life and normal routines are disrupted.
- Even functional objects are now capable of emotion.
- i.e. Not looking for a conventional way out.
- Now it's specific to her personally.
- Hands could represent creativity.
- It's looking for freedom — breaking away from its usual identity.
- The bed leaves darkness behind, in favour of enlightenment.
- Dramatic loudness, and again improbable because clouds aren't solid.
- It seemed unlikely until the moment it happened.
- Food is personified — everything is coming alive.
- More upward movement, to an unlikely height.
- Related to being grounded. But she's no longer "attached" to them — she's floating.
- Excitement and congratulation.
- Her hands have broken free.

Section One — The Poems

This Room

"This Room" is about a <u>special event</u> going on in the poet's life, which frees her from the restrictions of everyday existence. She metaphorically <u>rises out</u> of normality and darkness, and into <u>unlikeliness</u> and <u>enlightenment</u>. Reminds me of that time I worked out where the teletext button is on my remote.

You've Got To Know What Happens in the Poem

Lines 1-9   The room breaks out of itself, looking for <u>light and freedom</u> (lines 1-5). Then the <u>bed</u> rises into the <u>sky</u>. The <u>chairs</u> clearly reckon this is a smart idea so they get in on the act too.

Lines 10-18   The poet says <u>how great it feels</u> when something that seems really <u>unlikely</u> suddenly happens (lines 10-13). <u>Everyday objects</u> like kitchen utensils and food <u>come alive</u> and make loads of noise to celebrate (lines 14-15).

Lines 19-22   It's all been such <u>fun</u> she feels that she's left her <u>feet</u> behind her, and her newly-freed <u>hands</u> are applauding her.

Learn About the Three Types of Language

1) **PERSONIFICATION** — items of <u>furniture</u> come to life (lines 1-9), showing how exciting life has become. Parts of her <u>body</u> become independent (20-22), symbolising her new found <u>freedom</u>.

2) **IMPROBABILITY** — whatever the event is, it clearly seemed very <u>unlikely</u> right until the moment it happened (line 13). This creates the feeling that there's a <u>sudden explosion</u> of happiness.

3) **MOVEMENT** — things move <u>upwards</u> (line 9) and expand <u>outwards</u> (2-3), to show how much <u>richer</u> and full of <u>variety</u> life suddenly is. There's a sense of escaping by being <u>outside</u> her body (line 21).

Remember the Feelings and Attitudes in the Poem

1) She's <u>excited</u> (line 19) about the special moment in her life when things suddenly change for the better.

2) She feels <u>joyful</u> and <u>overwhelmed</u> because it's all so sudden and <u>improbable</u> (lines 10-11).

3) She's <u>relieved</u> that she's finally free (line 22).

Think About Your Feelings and Attitudes to the Poem

1) Pick 2 words or phrases that <u>stand out to you</u>. If none stand out, just pick 2 <u>unusual words or phrases</u>.

2) Write these 2 words or phrases down. Then write about how they <u>make you feel</u>. If they don't make you feel anything, don't worry — just <u>make something up</u>, as long as it's <u>not too stupid</u>.

> **EXAMPLE**   When the poet says "This is the time and place / to be alive", I'm filled with optimism. It makes me realise that anything is possible, right here and now.

This might seem over the top, but examiners want you to sound enthusiastic. So try and stick in something like this occasionally, even if you don't really mean it.

You have to use your imagination

Well, it's nice to have a <u>cheery</u> poem for a change eh? But what makes this one tricky is that it's <u>not specific</u> about what it's all about — it's just generally about something pretty cool going on. So you can be imaginative — think of an <u>event in your life</u> and relate it to the poem.

Section One — The Poems

Moniza Alvi

> She likes the Pakistani clothes, but can't feel attached to them. She's also trying to see her identity.

> The schoolfriend's reaction to the clothes contrasts with the poet's — so the poet doesn't entirely fit in in England either.

40 My salwar kameez
         didn't impress the schoolfriend
    who sat on my bed, asked to see
         my weekend clothes.
    But often I admired the mirror-work,
45   tried to glimpse myself
              in the miniature
    glass circles, recall the story
         how the three of us
              sailed to England.
50 Prickly heat had me screaming on the way.
         I ended up in a cot
    in my English grandmother's dining-room,
         found myself alone,
              playing with a tin boat.
55 I pictured my birthplace
         from fifties' photographs.
              When I was older
    there was conflict, a fractured land
         throbbing through newsprint.
60 Sometimes I saw Lahore –
              my aunts in shaded rooms,
    screened from male visitors,
         sorting presents,
              wrapping them in tissue.
65 Or there were beggars, sweeper-girls
         and I was there –
              of no fixed nationality,
    staring through fretwork
         at the Shalimar Gardens.

> The real boat took her away from her homeland.

> She must have been very young when she left Pakistan for England.

> She can't remember Pakistan properly — she has to imagine it.

> This refers to the war when East Pakistan split to become Bangladesh.

> The split in Pakistan is compared to her confused identity, split between England and Pakistan.

> Her knowledge of Pakistan is based on what she's read and heard.

> Brings the poem back to the original theme.

> Less positive images of Pakistan.

> Sums up her feeling of not being totally English or Pakistani.

> There's a barrier stopping her from being part of Pakistan.

POEM DICTIONARY
salwar kameez — Pakistani items of clothing
filigree — delicate gold jewellery
mirror work — a way of decorating clothing using sequins
Lahore — a city in Pakistan
Shalimar Gardens — peaceful, walled gardens in Lahore

Section One — The Poems

Moniza Alvi

Moniza Alvi was born in Pakistan in 1954, to a Pakistani father and an English mother. She moved to England as a child, and revisited Pakistan for the first time in 1993.

Presents from my Aunts in Pakistan

> *These words stand out from the English words, just as the presents do from the English clothes she usually wears.*

They sent me a salwar kameez
    peacock-blue,
        and another
glistening like an orange split open,
5 embossed slippers, gold and black
    points curling.
Candy-striped glass bangles
    snapped, drew blood.
Like at school, fashions changed
10 in Pakistan —
the salwar bottoms were broad and stiff,
    then narrow.
My aunts chose an apple-green sari,
    silver-bordered
15   for my teens.

I tried each satin-silken top —
    was alien in the sitting-room.
I could never be as lovely
    as those clothes —
20 I longed
for denim and corduroy.
    My costume clung to me
    and I was aflame,
I couldn't rise up out of its fire,
25   half-English,
      unlike Aunt Jamila.

I wanted my parents' camel-skin lamp —
    switching it on in my bedroom,
to consider the cruelty
30   and the transformation
from camel to shade,
    marvel at the colours
      like stained glass.

My mother cherished her jewellery —
35 Indian gold, dangling, filigree.
    But it was stolen from our car.
The presents were radiant in my wardrobe.
    My aunts requested cardigans
      from Marks and Spencers.

Annotations:
- *The bright colours of the Pakistani clothes contrast with the clothes she's used to (line 21).*
- *They broke — like her links with Pakistan.*
- *The presents make her feel out of place in England.*
- *She's more comfortable with the plainness of English clothes than the bright colours of the salwar kameez.*
- *Child-like desire for something she can't have.*
- *Refers to the legend of the Phoenix rising from the flames — but she can't re-create herself like this.*
- *The poet feels sorry for the camel whose skin was used to make the lamp. This reflects her own negative feelings about change.*
- *The theft of her mother's jewellery in England could be a metaphor for England stealing her Pakistani identity.*
- *Humorous but regretful — she never wore them.*

Section One — The Poems

THIS IS A FLAP.
FOLD THIS PAGE OUT.

Presents from my Aunts in Pakistan

A teenage girl who's grown up in England describes the presents she's received from relatives in Pakistan. Despite thinking the clothes and jewellery are beautiful, she feels uncomfortable wearing them. This makes her start thinking about Pakistan and wondering about her mixed identity.

You've Got To Know What Happens in the Poem

Lines 1-26	The poet remembers the clothes her aunts sent her when she was a teenager. When she tried them on, she didn't feel right in them — she thought they were too nice for her (lines 19-20).
Lines 27-43	She thinks of times when the cultures clashed, like the way she felt when her mum's jewellery was stolen, how she never wore the clothes from her aunts, and how her friend didn't like the presents.
Lines 44-69	The poet tries to make sense of the vague memories she has of first coming to England (lines 48-54), and of Pakistan (lines 55-65). She seems to think she'll never feel properly Pakistani or English.

Learn About the Three Types of Language

1) **CONFLICT** — Pakistan and England seem to contrast in every possible way, e.g. the bright colours of the salwar kameez are starkly different from the subdued Western clothes she prefers to wear.

2) **PAIN and UNCERTAINTY** — her lack of knowledge about the country where she was born (lines 55-59) causes her emotional turmoil. She feels uncomfortable when she tries on the Pakistani clothes. At the end of the poem, she feels isolated and excluded.

3) **METAPHORICAL LANGUAGE** — the poet uses metaphors like the situation in Pakistan (line 58) to reflect her own conflict over not quite fitting in.

Remember the Feelings and Attitudes in the Poem

1) There are memories of feeling confused and out of place as a teenager (lines 16-19).
2) The poet has mixed feelings about the presents and about Pakistan — she finds them attractive and exotic (line 44), but also foreign and strange (line 32).
3) She still feels uncertain of her identity at the end of the poem — she seems to feel like an outsider (lines 67-69).

Think About Your Feelings and Attitudes to the Poem

1) Pick 2 words or phrases that stand out to you. If none stand out, just pick 2 unusual words or phrases.
2) Write these 2 words or phrases down. Then write about how they make you feel. If they don't make you feel anything, don't worry — just make something up, as long as it's not too stupid.

> **EXAMPLE** When the poet describes herself as "of no fixed nationality", I feel sorry for her, as I have struggled to work out my own identity. The uncertain tone she has at the end of the poem suggests she is still struggling to resolve her dilemma.

Talk about unresolved conflict

Phew, this poem's a bit of a long 'un. But that's good because there's loads you can get out of it. Like a lot of the poems, it ends on a bit of an uncertain note, so you could write about why you think she's failed to solve her identity crisis. In fact, I'm certain you should do that. Kind of.

Section One — The Poems

Niyi Osundare

Niyi Osundare was born in Nigeria in 1947, and is a Professor of English. He has often spoken out against military regimes in his home country.

Not my Business

They picked Akanni up one morning
Beat him soft like clay
And stuffed him down the belly
Of a waiting jeep.
        5   What business of mine is it
               So long they don't take the yam
               From my savouring mouth?

They came one night
Booted the whole house awake
10 And dragged Danladi out,
Then off to a lengthy absence.
               What business of mine is it
               So long they don't take the yam
               From my savouring mouth?

15 Chinwe went to work one day
Only to find her job was gone:
No query, no warning, no probe –
Just one neat sack for a stainless record.
               What business of mine is it
20   So long they don't take the yam
               From my savouring mouth?

And then one evening
As I sat down to eat my yam
A knock on the door froze my hungry hand.
25 The jeep was waiting on my bewildered lawn
Waiting, waiting in its usual silence.

Annotations:

- *This line emphasises the brutality of his beating.* (Beat him soft like clay)
- *He uses first names — it's his friends who are being abused.* (Akanni)
- *The jeep is seen as an animal devouring him.* (stuffed him down the belly)
- *They violently and noisily disturb the sleeping household.* (Booted the whole house awake)
- *It seems that these are common occurrences.* (one night)
- *Using exactly the same words could show that it's an instinctive response — he doesn't want to think about it.* (refrain)
- *There's an ironically innocent sound to this — her job hasn't really just disappeared.* (her job was gone)
- *They don't have to answer to anyone — they can do what they like.* (No query, no warning, no probe)
- *Chinwe's treatment isn't violent, but it's still horribly unfair.*
- *The simple, factual tone makes it sound inevitable.* (Just one neat sack for a stainless record.)
- *Related to the refrain, but now it seems he'll be denied his yam — he's no longer unaffected.* (As I sat down to eat my yam / A knock on the door froze my hungry hand.)
- *Use of "the" shows it's the same jeep — so presumably he's in for the same treatment as Akanni.*
- *Menacing, like a predator.* (Waiting, waiting in its usual silence.)
- *Personification of the lawn stands for the speaker's own frightened confusion.* (bewildered lawn)

POEM DICTIONARY
yam — vegetable eaten in hot countries

Not my Business

Another rather bleak one, I'm afraid. From the point of view of an <u>African man</u>, the poet describes how various people in his neighbourhood are <u>mistreated</u>, probably by the secret police or the army. The narrator says that as long as he's left alone, it's <u>none of his business</u>. Then they come for him.

You've Got To Know What Happens in the Poem

Lines 1-14	A man called Akanni is <u>beaten up</u> and bundled into a <u>jeep</u> (lines 1-4). Then another man, Danladi, is <u>taken from his house</u> and isn't seen for ages (lines 8-11). After each incident, the narrator says that, as long as he's OK, he's <u>not getting involved</u> (lines 5-7, 12-14).
Lines 15-21	A woman called Chinwe discovers that she's been <u>sacked for no reason</u> (lines 15-18). Again the narrator says that it's <u>no business of his</u> (19-21).
Lines 22-26	As he sits down to eat, he hears a <u>knock on the door</u>. He's dead <u>scared</u> (lines 24). He looks outside and sees the jeep <u>waiting for him</u> (25-26). Uh-oh...

Learn About the Two Types of Language

1) **NARRATIVE VOICE** — the poet adopts the <u>persona</u> of a passive onlooker who thinks he <u>won't be affected</u> by the violence. This adds to the <u>impact</u> at the end when it <u>does</u> happen to him.

2) **VIOLENT LANGUAGE** — the brutality of the regime is shown by comparisons with <u>savage animals</u> (lines 3 and 26). The regime can get away with being <u>openly barbaric</u>, because people are so scared of it.

> *The last verse doesn't have the usual refrain about not caring — the speaker's voice has been silenced. The poet shows the speaker's attitude is flawed, as no one is safe under this kind of regime.*

Remember the Feelings and Attitudes in the Poem

1) The speaker says that what happens to other people <u>isn't his problem</u>.
2) But he's <u>scared</u> when it looks like the same thing will happen to him (line 24).
3) The way the poet describes the abuses (e.g. lines 2 and 17) shows he's actually very <u>angry</u> about them.
4) The message is that you <u>shouldn't ignore</u> these abuses, or one day it'll happen to you too. He thinks people should <u>stand up</u> against oppressive regimes.

Think About Your Feelings and Attitudes to the Poem

1) Pick 2 words or phrases that <u>stand out to you</u>. If none stand out, just pick 2 <u>unusual words or phrases</u>.
2) Write these 2 words or phrases down. Then write about how they <u>make you feel</u>. If they don't make you feel anything, don't worry — just <u>make something up</u>, as long as it's <u>not too stupid</u>.

> **EXAMPLE** The repeated phrase "my savouring mouth" makes me feel angry with the speaker, as he seems greedy and selfish. He turns a blind eye, and seems more interested in eating than in defending his friends.

Think about the poet's reasons for writing the poem

"Not my Business" isn't just a violent story — it's a <u>rallying call</u> to people living under brutal regimes to stop ignoring the situation and <u>stand up for themselves</u>. In your exam, you could write about how <u>effective</u> you think the poem is in doing this, and why.

Section One — The Poems

Grace Nichols

Grace Nichols was born in Guyana in 1950. She now lives and writes in Sussex.

Hurricane Hits England

It took a hurricane, to bring her closer
To the landscape.
Half the night she lay awake,
The howling ship of the wind,
5   Its gathering rage,
Like some dark ancestral spectre.
Fearful and reassuring.

Talk to me Huracan
Talk to me Oya
10 Talk to me Shango
And Hattie,
My sweeping, back-home cousin.

Tell me why you visit
An English coast?
15 What is the meaning
Of old tongues
Reaping havoc
In new places?

The blinding illumination,
20 Even as you short-
Circuit us
Into further darkness?

What is the meaning of trees
Falling heavy as whales
25 Their crusted roots
Their cratered graves?

O why is my heart unchained?

Tropical Oya of the Weather,
I am aligning myself to you,
30 I am following the movement of your winds,
I am riding the mystery of your storm.

Ah, sweet mystery,
Come to break the frozen lake in me,
Shaking the foundations of the very trees within me,
35 Come to let me know
That the earth is the earth is the earth.

Section One — The Poems

Hurricane Hits England

In 1987, southern England was hit by a <u>massive storm</u> that caused loads of damage. This makes the poet think of the hurricanes that regularly happen in the <u>Caribbean</u>, and she feels <u>spiritually connected</u> to both the Caribbean and England as a result. Which is nice.

You've Got To Know What Happens in the Poem

Lines 1-7   A woman is described lying in bed listening to the <u>raging storm</u>. She finds it both <u>scary and comforting</u> at the same time (line 7).

Lines 8-26   She asks the <u>storm gods</u> why they're visiting England when they usually stick to the Caribbean. She asks why they've uprooted so many massive old <u>trees</u>.

Lines 27-36   She <u>joins together</u> with the gods and feels herself <u>riding along</u> with them. She feels <u>liberated</u> by the experience, and she's <u>less homesick</u> afterwards.

Learn About the Three Types of Language

1) **MYTHICAL LANGUAGE** — the poet uses beliefs from the Yorubans in <u>Africa</u> about the weather being <u>controlled by gods</u>. Although these gods are scary, she sees them as positive and <u>well-meaning</u>, and talks to them in respectful, <u>dramatic language</u>, e.g. lines 29-31.

2) **POWERFUL LANGUAGE** — there are lots of metaphors and similes to show how <u>devastating</u> the effects of the storm are, e.g. line 24, where the <u>trees</u> are compared to <u>beached whales</u>.

3) **PHILOSOPHICAL LANGUAGE** — at the start she feels like she's <u>a long way from home</u>. But the hurricane makes her think about whether where she lives is <u>actually important</u> or not (line 36).

Remember the Feelings and Attitudes in the Poem

1) At first she's <u>scared</u> by the storm (lines 5-7).
2) Then she makes the connection with the gods, and seems <u>angry</u> with them for coming to England (lines 13-18). There's a tone of <u>indignation</u> in her questions.
3) But then she feels a <u>connection</u> with the storm, and finds <u>meaning</u> in it — she sees it as a <u>link with nature</u> and with the Caribbean.
4) She's <u>grateful</u> to the storm — she thinks it's come to help her (line 33).

Think About Your Feelings and Attitudes to the Poem

1) I bet you think I'm going to tell you to pick 2 words or phrases that <u>stand out to you</u>, don't you?
2) And then to write them down and say how they <u>make you feel</u> and everything. Well I'm not. You should darn well <u>know all that</u> by now. Although technically, I suppose, I just have. Damn.

> **EXAMPLE**   When the poet refers to the storm as "some dark ancestral spectre", it makes me feel that there's something contradictory about it: the "spectre" sounds menacing, but the word "ancestral" shows that it is linked to her roots, so it could also be seen as comforting.

It's another one about culture and identity

Now this is what I call a poem — loads of <u>dramatic</u> talk about lightning and storm gods, and plenty of cracking <u>metaphors</u> to get stuck into. Top stuff. Just remember it's about more than storms — it shares the <u>cultural theme</u> with several other poems, and that's what Section 2's about...

Section One — The Poems

Identity

Identity in these poems is about <u>who we are</u> and what has made us like this.

1) It's about being young or old, <u>male or female</u>, rich or poor, powerful or weak, <u>white or black</u>, victim or tyrant, confident or uncertain, <u>religious</u> or not.
2) It's also about <u>where you come from</u>. Which country, region, background and political system you're from.
3) Other aspects also determine your identity — your <u>language</u>, your <u>family</u>, your <u>customs</u>, your <u>religion</u>, your <u>history</u> and <u>past experiences</u>. They're all part of the individual that you are.

Identity is What we Think of Ourselves

Search for My Tongue (Pages 18-19)
1) The poet is fluent in two languages, but the English, "foreign", tongue <u>dominates</u>.
2) She's worried that she has <u>lost her mother tongue</u>, which she feels is part of her <u>identity</u>.
3) She's <u>relieved</u> when she realises that her mother tongue, Gujarati, is strong and will <u>always be there</u>.

Hurricane Hits England (Pages 32-33)
1) The storm <u>awakens the poet</u> from her "frozen" state.
2) She has settled in England but does not feel completely <u>at home</u>.
3) The <u>violence of the storm</u> reminds her of her home in the Caribbean, and her <u>ancestral roots</u> in Africa.
4) She regains her sense of identity, and makes <u>connections</u> between England and her homeland. She realises that the Earth is a <u>whole</u>, and that we should never feel cut off from our roots.

Presents from my Aunts in Pakistan (Pages 28-29)
1) The teenager is <u>confused</u> about her identity as she is split between being Pakistani and being English.
2) All the exotic clothes sent by her aunts <u>attract</u> her, but they also <u>embarrass</u> her.
3) She <u>never resolves</u> her identity in the poem.

Identity is What Others Think of Us

Nothing's Changed (Pages 4-5)
1) This poem traces the anger of a <u>South African</u> man when he returns to the area he used to live in.
2) Although apartheid has been abolished, <u>inequalities</u> between different races <u>remain</u>.
3) So the poet's <u>identity</u> is partly imposed on him by <u>other people</u> — he's treated as a <u>second-class citizen</u> because of his <u>colour</u>.

Unrelated Incidents (Pages 20-21)
1) The poet is angry that his Glaswegian dialect is not taken seriously or <u>trusted in society</u>.
2) The poem shows us that we'd be <u>shocked to hear the news</u> read in this way — we're used to an <u>educated accent</u> telling us the "truth" of the news.
3) So the poem shows us that <u>dialect</u> can be part of identity, because society sometimes <u>judges</u> people by the way they <u>speak</u>.

The poet's sense of identity puts the poem in context

'Love After Love' (24-25), 'This Room' (26-27), and 'Limbo' (2-3) also talk about <u>identity</u>. In some poems, like 'Presents from my Aunts', it's the poet's <u>main reason</u> for writing. It's important to understand the poet's sense of identity, as it can explain <u>why they feel</u> like they do.

Section Two — The Themes

Politics

Politics means how a country is run, and how a government treats its citizens.
Politics affects both society as a whole and individual people.

> 1) Politics can be about the differences between rich and poor.
> 2) It can be about how leaders use and abuse their power.
> 3) Politics can be about certain groups gaining power and oppressing other groups.

Politics is about Inequality

Nothing's Changed (Pages 4-5)
1) It's set in Nelson Mandela's new South African democracy — apartheid has been officially abolished.
2) But the poet finds that there are still inequalities — the "whites only inn" won't accept him because of his colour, so he has to go to the grimy "working man's cafe".
3) So there are two kinds of inequality here — how much money you have, and what race you are.

Two Scavengers in a Truck... (Pages 10-11)
1) The gap between the rich and poor is very clear.
2) The USA prides itself on equal opportunity for all — but here we're shown the "gulf" that exists between the "casually coifed" young woman and the "grungy" garbagemen.
3) The poet condemns this failure in the political system.

Vultures (Pages 14-15)
1) The Commandant represents Nazi Germany's abuse of power — the Nazis murdered millions of Jews because they believed in the racial superiority of white, "Aryan" people.
2) This destruction of another culture and race was government policy.

"If I ever get my hands on that barber..."

It's about People's Attitudes and Opinions

What Were They Like? (Pages 16-17)
1) Many people were against America's involvement in the Vietnam War in the 1960s and 1970s.
2) The poet shows her opposition to the war by describing an extreme vision of the future, where all Vietnamese culture has been wiped out by the shock and violence of the war.

Unrelated Incidents (Pages 20-21)
1) "Unrelated Incidents" is about the power that language holds. The poet says a Glaswegian accent delivering the news would not be believed or respected.
2) The political dimension here involves us all and the judgements we make about people because of how they speak. Certain accents are associated with authority, others are treated as inferior.

You don't have to be Jeremy Paxman

Don't panic if your knowledge of world politics is a bit scratchy. It can help to know the odd fact, but you can work a lot out just from the poems — so don't go thinking you have to know the complete socio-political history of Nigeria. It's an English exam, not Politics.

Section Two — The Themes

Change

Some of the poems deal with a <u>change</u> in the poet's life, or in the world. This can be a change of <u>circumstance</u> or a change in <u>personality</u>, and it can be positive or negative.

> 1) People can experience a change which <u>frees them</u> from their problems.
> 2) Things can change for the <u>worse</u> — on a temporary or permanent basis.
> 3) Things may <u>appear</u> to have changed but in fact be very <u>similar</u> to how they always were.

Things can Change for the Better

Search For My Tongue (Pages 18-19)
1) The poet is worried that she's <u>lost her mother tongue</u> (Gujarati) because her "foreign" tongue (English) has taken over.
2) A <u>positive change</u> occurs when she dreams in Gujarati and realises it will <u>always be with her</u>.
3) This change is <u>internal</u> and <u>personal</u>.

This Room (Pages 26-27)
1) This poem is about a <u>sudden and unexpected change</u> in the poet's life.
2) We <u>don't know exactly</u> what this change is.
3) But it's clearly a <u>positive</u> one, that will affect her life in a <u>massive</u> way — "this is the time and place / to be alive".

Found it

Change can be a Bad Thing

What Were They Like? (Pages 16-17)
1) The poet describes a <u>negative change</u> — the traditional Vietnamese culture has been <u>destroyed</u>.
2) It seems like this is a <u>permanent loss</u>. The poem concludes with, "It is silent now".

Presents from my Aunts in Pakistan (Pages 28-29)
1) In this poem, the poet is <u>afraid of change</u> — trying to wear clothes she's not used to makes her <u>uncomfortable</u>.
2) This causes her way of <u>thinking about herself</u> to change. She now has to confront <u>both sides</u> of her background, whereas before she had <u>ignored</u> her Pakistani roots.
3) She also mentions a <u>change in the past</u>, i.e. when she first came to England from Pakistan as a small child. This change is what has <u>led to the current situation</u>.

Nothing's Changed (Pages 4-5)
1) In between the poet's last visit to District Six and the visit he describes in the poem, there's been a major <u>political change</u> — apartheid has been abolished.
2) In theory, this is a <u>positive</u> change, as all races are now <u>officially equal</u>.
3) But, in terms of <u>attitudes</u> and the <u>way people live</u>, the poet says that things <u>haven't changed</u> at all — non-white people are still treated as inferior.

Some poets call for change, others criticise it

It's a fairly open topic, so there are loads of <u>angles</u> you could tackle it from. The changes described in any two of the poems on this page will have things <u>in common</u> and things that are <u>different</u>.

Section Two — The Themes

People

The poems talk about the lives of both <u>individuals</u> and <u>groups</u> of people.

> 1) Some poets are interested in <u>society</u>, and people's attitudes towards, and treatment of, each other.
> 2) Sometimes one <u>group</u> of people live a completely <u>different lifestyle</u> from that of another group.
> 3) Others are interested in people who are <u>on their own</u>, and get on with things as <u>individuals</u>.

People are Affected by Society

Half-Caste (Pages 22-23)
1) The <u>words</u> people use can show the <u>attitudes</u> they have towards different groups in society.
2) The poet says the term "half-caste" is a <u>silly</u> and <u>offensive</u> way of describing mixed-race people.
3) He <u>challenges</u> people to <u>reassess</u> how they see each other.

Not my Business (Pages 30-31)
1) The poet shows how <u>terrible</u> it is to be ruled by a violent regime.
2) He says that if people <u>ignore</u> what's happening to their neighbours, things will get worse and eventually <u>everyone</u> will suffer.
3) He encourages people to <u>stand up</u> for each other, in order to create a <u>better society</u>.

Two Scavengers in a Truck... (Pages 10-11)
1) There's a clear <u>division</u> between the two pairs of people in the poem.
2) The scavengers can only <u>stare</u> at the couple in the Merc and <u>imagine</u> what it would be like to live like them — they can never cross the "small gulf" between them.
3) The poet <u>criticises American society</u> for not doing anything about this <u>social divide</u>. His reference to "democracy" is sarcastic.

Some People are On Their Own

Island Man (Pages 6-7)
1) This poem is about an <u>individual</u> who feels on his own.
2) The man in "Island Man" has a clear sense of <u>where he belongs</u>, i.e. in the Caribbean, not in London.
3) It's a fairly straightforward and familiar story of being <u>homesick</u>.

Hurricane Hits England (Pages 32-33)
1) Although <u>millions</u> of people were affected by the 1987 storm, the poet in "Hurricane Hits England" talks about her own <u>personal experience</u> of it.
2) The storm triggers a <u>moment of realisation</u> that changes the way she approaches life.
3) The storm makes her see that it <u>doesn't make sense</u> to feel homesick, because all parts of the Earth are <u>connected</u> to each other.

We are all individuals (apart from me)

'Presents from my Aunts' (pages 28-29), 'Night of the Scorpion' (12-13) and 'Vultures' (14-15) are also good poems for this topic. All the people in these poems encounter <u>problems</u> of some sort — you could compare someone who <u>solves their problems</u> with someone who <u>can't</u>, and discuss why.

Section Two — The Themes

First Person

If a poet writes in the first person, they use words like "I" and "me", rather than "she" or "him".

> 1) Writing in the first person allows the poet to use their voice directly.
> 2) This allows them to say how they feel and what they mean.
> 3) The first person lets us see things from the poet or character's point of view.

Some Poets "Look Inside Themselves"

Presents from my Aunts in Pakistan (Pages 28-29)

1) The first person perspective in this poem lets us see how confused and uncertain the girl is.
2) Phrases like "I could never be as lovely / as those clothes" (lines 18-19) give us an insight into her emotions that wouldn't be possible without the first person style.

Search For My Tongue (Pages 18-19)

1) The poet uses a conversational tone ("You ask me what I mean"), so that it sounds like she's explaining her thoughts to you, as if you're a friend.
2) Her descriptions of her dreams give us an idea of how her mind works.
3) This is important to the idea that her mother tongue is living inside her.

"You can't have mine"

This Room (Pages 26-27)

1) The poem's about a very personal experience.
2) The poet uses the first person perspective to show us how important the event is to her.
3) Surreal images like her hands being "outside, clapping" show the weird feelings she's experiencing.

Some Poets Want to Inform or Persuade People

Nothing's Changed (Pages 4-5)

1) The poet's voice allows us to experience the inequality through his eyes.
2) He sees the luxury of the whites only inn — "I press my nose / to the clear panes" (lines 27-28) — but knows he's not welcome there.
3) He wants us to realise how unfair it is.
4) Using the first person makes his message more effective.

Not my Business (Pages 30-31)

1) The poet adopts the persona of a man who doesn't get involved when people are abused.
2) He shows the selfishness of this attitude — "What business of mine is it...?"
3) By showing that this mentality is flawed, the poet tries to convince people to do the opposite of what the man does, and stand up for each other.

Night of the Scorpion (Pages 12-13)

1) We see events unfold through the eyes of a child — "I watched the holy man perform his rites" (line 42).
2) He's scared and confused by the religious response to his mother being stung by the scorpion.
3) The poet uses the first person to show how confusing and illogical this response seems to him. He sees it as superstitious and unhelpful.

The first person lets the poet speak directly to the reader

'Limbo' (pages 2-3) 'Half-Caste' (pages 22-23) and 'Hurricane...' (32-33) also use the first person. It makes a massive difference to the effect of the poem, as it lets the poet talk personally — poems like "Not my Business" would really lose their impact if it was just "he" or "she" instead of "I".

Section Two — The Themes

Specific Cultural References

Culture can be described as all the things which make up a community's <u>way of life</u>. Specific cultural references include beliefs, customs, religions, history, literature and loads of other things.

> 1) There can be <u>different cultures</u> within the <u>same society</u>.
> 2) Some people can grow up <u>surrounded</u> by a particular culture <u>without</u> really feeling <u>part of it</u>.
> 3) Some cultures <u>classify</u> people according to things like <u>race</u>, <u>gender</u> and <u>wealth</u>, rather than believing that everyone is equal.

Some Cultures are Divided

Two Scavengers in a Truck... (Pages 10-11)
1) The <u>language</u> of the poem, e.g. "downtown" and "garbage truck", is strongly associated with <u>American culture</u>.
2) The culture of the USA claims to value <u>equal opportunity</u> and <u>democracy</u>.
3) But it seems like the binmen will <u>never be able</u> to live like the rich couple.
4) So the <u>image</u> we have of American culture, where supposedly "everything is always possible" (line 30), is shown to be <u>false</u>.

This culture isn't featured

Nothing's Changed (Pages 4-5)
1) The culture here is the divided society of modern <u>South Africa</u>. The poet mentions that it's District Six because this is the area he knows, but it applies to the <u>whole country</u>.
2) The idea of <u>racial segregation</u> is familiar when thinking of the country under apartheid, but the fact that it <u>still exists</u> under Mandela's rule seems <u>shocking</u>.
3) There's the odd use of South African <u>slang</u>, such as "boy" and "bunny chows", which adds to the feel of the poem being relevant <u>specifically</u> to South Africa.

Limbo (Pages 2-3)
1) The theme here is <u>slavery</u>. Although it was abolished in the 19th Century, the <u>history</u> of slavery is still <u>important</u> to many black people today.
2) There are references to life as a slave, such as the <u>cramped conditions</u> on the slave ships.
3) The <u>limbo dance</u> is strongly linked to this West Indian slave culture.

People can Become Separated from their Culture

Night of the Scorpion (Pages 12-13)
1) It's set in a <u>Hindu</u> community in India.
2) The locals believe in <u>reincarnation</u>. The prayers relate to <u>purifying the soul</u> for the next life.
3) But the boy's father is a "sceptic", so the boy's probably grown up in a <u>non-religious</u> household — which must make the Hindu ceremony seem very <u>odd</u>.

Hurricane Hits England (Pages 32-33)
1) Before the storm, the poet has been feeling like an <u>outsider</u> to English culture.
2) She refers to African <u>storm gods</u> — Huracan, Oya and Shango.
3) The poet uses these as a link to her <u>Caribbean roots</u> — black Caribbeans were originally from Africa.

Culture can be the central theme or provide the setting

'What Were They Like?' (pages 16-17), 'Search For My Tongue' (18-19), 'Not my Business' (30-31), and 'Presents from my Aunts' (28-29) also fit into this topic. There are loads of <u>different cultures</u> in the anthology, which means there's plenty of <u>variety</u> to keep you <u>on your toes</u>.

Section Two — The Themes

Description

Poets use various ways of <u>describing</u> things to keep the reader <u>interested</u>.

> 1) Poets can use exciting or unexpected <u>adjectives</u> to describe things or people.
> 2) They can use <u>comparisons</u>, strong <u>opinions</u> or <u>humour</u> if they want to give a particular <u>impression</u> of something or someone.
> 3) Contrasting descriptions can be used to show <u>differences</u> between people or places.

Poets Describe People

Two Scavengers in a Truck... (Pages 10-11)

1) There's a sharp <u>contrast</u> between the <u>appearances</u> of the "grungy" binmen and the "elegant couple".
2) There's also a <u>suggested</u> contrast between <u>how hard</u> the two pairs of people <u>work</u> — the "scavengers" have been "up since 4 a.m.", while the driver of the Mercedes is still "on his way" to work.
3) <u>Contradictory</u> descriptions of the rich couple sometimes suggest <u>falseness</u> or <u>dishonesty</u>, e.g. "casually coifed" — "coifing" suggests time and effort, so the woman's casual image is <u>fake</u>.

Presents from my Aunts in Pakistan (Pages 28-29)

1) The poet's descriptions of the <u>presents</u> show her mixed feelings.
2) They're "<u>lovely</u>" but also "<u>broad and stiff</u>", showing they're <u>uncomfortable</u>.
3) Similes such as "glistening like an orange" show they also seem <u>exotic</u> to her, rather than normal.
4) Descriptions of <u>one thing</u> often also apply to <u>another</u>, e.g. Pakistan is "fractured", like her identity.

Blessing (Pages 8-9)

1) The descriptions of the <u>rush for water</u> from the burst pipe show how <u>desperate</u> the people are.
2) They have "frantic hands", which shows the <u>urgency</u> with which they collect the water.
3) The water is described as "fortune" and "silver", showing how <u>valuable</u> it is.
4) <u>Basic items</u> like "tin mugs" and "plastic buckets" seem to be the only possessions they own and they live in "huts" which emphasises how <u>poor</u> the slum-dwellers are.

Poets Describe Places

Nothing's Changed (Pages 4-5)

1) The poet's descriptions of "hard stones", "seeding grasses" and "amiable weeds" in the first verse give an impression of District Six being <u>neglected</u> and <u>run-down</u>.
2) The <u>differences</u> between the lives of whites and blacks are shown by the contrast between the "<u>haute cuisine</u>" at the "up-market" inn and the "<u>bunny chows</u>" eaten at "a plastic table's top" at the cafe.

"You're not having my chows"

Island Man (Pages 6-7)

1) The "emerald island" of the Caribbean, with its "wild seabirds", sounds like an <u>unspoilt paradise</u>.
2) By contrast, the "grey metallic soar" of London traffic sounds <u>dreary and unnatural</u>.
3) We only hear the <u>good things about the Caribbean</u> and the <u>bad things about London</u>, which makes us realise he's longing to be back home.

Compare the different descriptions in a poem

Poets use descriptions to make their poems more interesting to read. Poets can use a lot of descriptions which <u>complement</u> each other to create an <u>overall impression</u> of something. But also look out for descriptions which <u>contrast</u> with something else in another part of the poem.

Section Two — The Themes

Metaphor

A <u>metaphor</u> is when something is described as if it's <u>something else</u> for effect.

> 1) Metaphors can be used to <u>emphasise</u> just how big, fast, fat, brilliant, rubbish or weird something or someone is.
> 2) <u>Extended</u> metaphors (also called <u>running</u> metaphors) are when a writer takes a metaphor and keeps going with it, applying <u>different aspects</u> of the metaphor to the thing being described.

Don't confuse metaphors with similes. A <u>simile</u> says something is <u>like</u> something else — a <u>metaphor</u> says it actually <u>is</u> something else.

Metaphors can Describe *People's Lives*

Vultures (Pages 14-15)

1) The vultures are ugly, <u>disgusting</u> creatures but they're still capable of <u>gentleness</u>.
2) This leads to the description of the Commandant, who <u>murders</u> people every day yet <u>loves his child</u>.
3) So the <u>vultures</u> are a metaphor for the Commandant — although we <u>don't realise</u> this at first, as more than half the poem has passed before the Commandant is mentioned.

Blessing (Pages 8-9)

1) Water is described as "fortune" and "silver", showing how <u>valuable</u> it is to the people of the slum.
2) The people become a "congregation", creating a <u>religious</u> feel — they're <u>worshipping</u> this gift from "a kindly god".
3) The metaphor "The blessing sings / over their small bones" (lines 1 and 23) to describe the burst water pipe reinforces the <u>miraculous</u> feel of the poem's title and how <u>vulnerable</u> the children are.

Metaphors can Describe *Feelings*

This Room (Pages 26-27)

1) The <u>room</u> and the <u>furniture</u> become <u>alive</u>. This shows how the poet feels suddenly <u>free</u> after the special event that's happened.
2) The fact that such <u>ordinary</u> objects are "rising up to crash through clouds" (line 9) shows how <u>extraordinary</u> the situation is.
3) At the end of the poem, individual <u>parts of the poet's body</u> become independent, living things — maybe showing how <u>dizzy</u> and <u>disoriented</u> she is by all the excitement.

Any second...NOW

Search For My Tongue (Pages 18-19)

1) The poet's <u>mother tongue</u> (Gujarati) is described as a <u>living thing</u> — she's worried that it will "rot and die".
2) This idea becomes a <u>running metaphor</u>. Gujarati is described metaphorically as a <u>flower</u>, and words like "bud" and "blossoms" show that it's <u>growing back</u>.
3) This creates the impression that her mother tongue is <u>rooted</u> in her.

Half-Caste (Pages 22-23)

1) The poet <u>mocks</u> the term "half-caste" by comparing mixed-race people to classical music and paintings — the idea of calling these things "half" just because they're mixed seems <u>absurd</u>.
2) He then uses the "half" idea to describe <u>body parts</u>, e.g. "I offer yu half-a-hand". This could be seen as a <u>metaphor</u> for the poet being <u>less than welcoming</u> to people with certain points of view.
3) He mixes in <u>humour</u> with his metaphors, so that his point about the <u>stupidity</u> of the word is clear.

Metaphors make poems more interesting

Remember to say <u>why</u> you think a poet has chosen to use a particular metaphor. Think about what <u>impression</u> the metaphor gives. If you can work this out, it's a big clue to the poet's <u>message</u>.

Section Two — The Themes

Unusual Presentation

A lot of these poems have an odd layout. This might look daft at first, but it can be effective.

> 1) The way a poem looks on the page affects your first impressions of it.
> 2) Regular styles of presentation tend to create a certain effect throughout the poem.
> 3) Irregular layout can create different effects in different parts of the poem.

Presentation can Create an Overall Effect

What Were They Like? (Pages 16-17)
1) The questions and answers are numbered so that it looks like a "real" enquiry.
2) Each question can be matched to its corresponding answer.
3) Each pair covers a particular aspect of the Vietnamese culture.
4) When you read a question and then its answer, meanings of certain words change subtly, e.g. "bone" in Q4 and A4 — this adds to the uncertain tone.
5) The failure to come up with any satisfactory answers adds to the sense of the poet's condemnation of the war.

Unrelated Incidents (Pages 20-21)
1) The short lines of almost even length make the poem look like a newsreader's autocue.
2) This adds humour to the poem, by creating a visual impression of the theme it discusses.
3) It's being read as if it's the news, so it sounds like the truth — the newsreader presents his views as fact rather than opinion.

Presentation can Allow for Different Effects

Limbo (Pages 2-3)
1) There's a lot of variance between line lengths — some lines are quite long, others are only one word.
2) The longer lines, e.g. line 7, create an impression of the ongoing cruelty of slave conditions.
3) Shorter lines describe movement, e.g. the repetition of "down" makes it feel like an ongoing descent.
4) The repeated "limbo like me" lines are in italics to emphasise the rhythm of the dance that is always in the background.

Search For My Tongue (Pages 18-19)
1) Seeing the Gujarati script allows us to see how different it is to English.
2) This gives us an insight into why it's so important to the poet — it represents a different side of her personality.
3) The Gujarati words are spelt out phonetically too, so we can hear what they sound like.

Presentation can reflect the poem's theme

'Two Scavengers in a Truck, Two Beautiful People in a Mercedes' (pages 10-11), and 'Presents from my Aunts in Pakistan' (28-29) also have unusual presentation. It's all about creating a visual effect, to add to the effect of the words and illustrate whatever point the poet is making.

Section Two — The Themes

Non-Standard English

Standard English means talking in a <u>posh</u> accent, using "correct" grammar and <u>no slang</u>.
So non-standard English means anything else.

1) Non-standard English can mean talking in a <u>regional accent</u>, like Scouse or Geordie.
2) It includes using different forms of <u>grammar</u>, like West Indian creole.
3) <u>Slang</u> words and <u>swearing</u> are non-standard English.
4) Non-standard English can mean being <u>creative</u> with the words you use.

Language Links a Poem with its Background

Limbo (Pages 2-3)
1) The poet uses the West Indian <u>creole</u> dialect that slaves spoke in.
2) This links the poem with <u>slave history</u>, and allows the poet to write from a <u>slave's point-of-view</u>.
3) The <u>simplified grammar</u> of creole gives the poem a <u>harsh</u> sound, e.g. "stick hit sound" — this adds to the impression of the <u>cruelty</u> of slave punishment.

Island Man (Pages 6-7)
1) Words are used in <u>unconventional</u> ways, creating a <u>confused feel</u> in the language.
2) "Wombing" is used to describe the gentle, <u>comforting sounds</u> of the sea, but it also connects the sea to the man's <u>birth</u>, showing it's where he <u>belongs</u>.
3) The word "sands" is used to show that he's still <u>thinking of the Caribbean</u>, even though he's living in London.
4) Some words could apply to aspects of life in <u>both the Caribbean and London</u>, e.g. "roar" is used to describe the London <u>traffic</u>, but it also sounds like the <u>sea</u>.

Dialect can be In-Yer-Face

Unrelated Incidents (Pages 20-21)
1) The whole poem is written <u>phonetically</u> to represent a <u>Glaswegian accent</u>.
2) This emphasises how <u>different</u> it sounds to standard English.
3) Dialect is the <u>subject</u> of the poem, so there's an <u>ironic</u> feel to putting an opinion that says regional accents are <u>inferior</u> into a <u>regional accent</u>.
4) The poet shows he's <u>not ashamed</u> to speak in his natural voice — he wants it to be <u>heard</u>, because he thinks we hear <u>enough posh accents</u> in public life.

Half-Caste (Pages 22-23)
1) The <u>West Indian dialect</u> sounds more <u>direct</u> than standard English, so the poet can <u>challenge</u> the reader, e.g. "wha yu mean".
2) Non-standard English allows the reader to "hear" the <u>poet's voice</u>, so it feels more like a <u>conversation</u>.
3) The <u>mixture</u> of standard and non-standard English reflects the poet's <u>mixed background</u>, and shows that he's proud of it.

De language adds to de effeck

With poems like 'Half-Caste', it's easy to think the poet's just <u>showing off</u> by writing in dialect. But the poems really wouldn't be very <u>effective</u> if they just said, "In my opinion, it's perfectly acceptable to speak in dialect," or something like that. The <u>sound</u> of the poem when <u>spoken</u> is vital.

Section Two — The Themes

Particular Places

The descriptions of <u>places</u> are strongly linked to the <u>message</u> of some of these poems.

> 1) Some poets describe their <u>homes</u> or <u>birthplaces</u>.
> 2) Other poets use a setting as a background for the <u>topic</u> they want to talk about.
> 3) Places aren't always described in detail — sometimes a <u>lack of detail</u> can be effective.

Places can be Connected to Identity

Presents from my Aunts in Pakistan (Pages 28-29)

1) The poet only <u>vaguely</u> remembers Pakistan — she relies on <u>photos</u> and <u>newspapers</u> to describe it.
2) Pakistan is described as "fractured", reflecting the poet's <u>split identity</u>.
3) The poet's <u>personal</u> memories of Pakistan are of <u>mysterious</u> "shaded rooms" and beggars.
4) These aren't very positive thoughts — she's <u>uncomfortable</u> with the idea of being Pakistani.

Hurricane Hits England (Pages 32-33)

1) The woman wants to feel "closer / To the landscape" — she feels <u>emotional</u> about places.
2) At the start of the poem, she feels a <u>long way</u> from her home in the Caribbean.
3) When England gets a taste of a Caribbean-style storm, it makes her realise that <u>everywhere on Earth is connected</u> — so places aren't that important after all.

Places can Stand for the State of Society

Two Scavengers in a Truck... (Pages 10-11)

1) It's San Francisco, though it could be <u>many places in America</u>.
2) The description of the setting in lines 1-2 sounds <u>unremarkable</u>, suggesting the situation the poet describes is not unusual — this is normal, <u>everyday life</u>.
3) The situation represents the poet's views on <u>America</u> in general, and the <u>inequalities</u> he sees in its capitalist "democracy".

Nothing's Changed (Pages 4-5)

1) Harsh-sounding descriptions of stones and weeds <u>set the tone</u> for the <u>bitterness</u> of the poem.
2) The poet instinctively <u>recognises</u> his home district — "my feet know / and my hands".
3) The <u>neglected</u> condition of District Six and the <u>segregation</u> that still exists there represent the situation in the <u>whole of South Africa</u>.
4) There's a clear <u>division</u> in one street — the plush inn at one end, and the grimy cafe, "down the road". This shows how the blacks and whites live <u>very close</u> to each other, but live <u>separate</u> lives.

Vultures (Pages 14-15)

1) Bleak descriptions of the <u>vultures' habitat</u> create a <u>dark, miserable mood</u>.
2) The poem starts at dawn, but there's only "greyness" and "drizzle" — there's <u>no sign of the sun</u>.
3) There's <u>no other life</u> in this place — just a "dead tree", introducing the theme of <u>death</u>.
4) The <u>dark, evil atmosphere</u> of the setting provides the perfect background for the <u>human evil</u> that the poem goes on to discuss.

Find out some bits and pieces about the setting

Often the setting is just a <u>backdrop</u> to the poem's issues. But in some poems, like 'Hurricane Hits England', it's the <u>main theme</u>, so it's useful to know a thing or two about these places.

Section Two — The Themes

Two Cultures

Some of the poets talk about the effects of having <u>two different cultures</u> in their lives.

> 1) Having a <u>mixed background</u> can make people feel like they're <u>torn</u> between two cultures.
> 2) Sometimes people have <u>moved</u> to a different country and <u>miss</u> the culture they're <u>used to</u>.
> 3) Some cultures are <u>divided</u>, with one sub-culture <u>dominating</u> another.

Some Cultures Clash

Search For My Tongue (Pages 18-19)

1) The poet sees the English and Asian cultures as being <u>separate parts of her</u>, that <u>can't</u> be brought together.
2) This <u>opposition</u> is shown through <u>languages</u> — her mother tongue (Gujarati) "could not really know the other" (English).
3) By the end of the poem, the two languages seem to be <u>fighting each other</u> — Gujarati "ties the other tongue in knots".

Unrelated Incidents (Pages 20-21)

1) The two cultures in this poem are <u>posh English</u> culture and <u>working-class Scottish</u> culture.
2) Again, the division is shown through <u>language</u> — standard BBC English versus regional accents. The poet believes that people <u>dismiss</u> regional accents as <u>inferior</u>.
3) The poet <u>stands up</u> for his own background, by criticising the <u>dominance</u> of English voices.

Presents from my Aunts in Pakistan (Pages 28-29)

1) The poet has spent most of her life in <u>England</u>, so the presents from <u>Pakistan</u> seem <u>foreign</u> to her, even though she was born in Pakistan and has relatives there.
2) The poet feels that the two cultures <u>don't mix well</u> — she feels "alien in the sitting-room" when she tries on the Pakistani clothes.
3) The realisation that she belongs to two cultures seems to <u>confuse</u> her rather than help her — at the end she seems to feel like an <u>outsider to both</u>.

Cultures can Mix Together

Half-Caste (Pages 22-23)

1) The poet in "Half-Caste" reckons cultures <u>can mix together</u>.
2) The theme is that it's <u>good</u> when <u>cultures mix</u> — he compares it to "when light an shadow / mix in de sky", suggesting it's <u>natural</u>.
3) The poet seems <u>proud</u> of his own <u>mixed background</u>.

Hurricane Hits England (Pages 32-33)

1) The woman in the poem <u>doesn't feel a part</u> of English culture — she misses the Caribbean.
2) At the start of the poem, the cultures seem very <u>different</u>, and she feels a <u>long way from home</u>.
3) By the end, thanks to the storm gods, the poet sees all places and cultures as <u>being connected</u>, and suggests the differences <u>aren't important</u> after all — "the earth is the earth is the earth".

Belonging to two cultures can be good or bad

The main difference between the ways the poets talk about having two cultures in their lives is that some <u>like it</u> and some <u>don't</u>. Remember that everyone's background is <u>different</u>, so it's <u>not</u> as simple as some of them moaning about it and some of them making the most of it.

Section Two — The Themes

Universal Ideas

If something's <u>universal</u>, it could apply to <u>any place or time</u>, rather than being restricted to the exact situation in the poem. Many of these poets deal with universal themes.

> 1) Ideas like <u>loneliness</u>, <u>equality</u> and <u>identity</u> have interested people all over the world for ages.
> 2) Some poets talk about a <u>specific situation</u> as a way of making a point about people or society <u>in general</u>.

Some Poets Talk About Equality

Half-Caste (Pages 22-23)
1) This poem deals with ideas of <u>inferiority</u> and <u>equality</u>.
2) The poet thinks the expression "half-caste" suggests mixed-race people are <u>inferior</u>.
3) He <u>challenges</u> this viewpoint, sarcastically saying that he casts "half-a-shadow".
4) He <u>turns the idea around</u> by saying that it's the people who use the term "half-caste" who are <u>incomplete</u> because they don't use "de whole of yu mind".

Two Scavengers in a Truck... (Pages 10-11)
1) The theme of this poem is how people allow <u>inequality</u> to happen.
2) As well as being a dig specifically at <u>American capitalist society</u>, we know that inequality occurs to some extent in <u>any society</u>.
3) We see how the garbagemen are <u>fascinated</u> with the rich people, but the rich couple <u>aren't interested</u> in the garbagemen.
4) This suggests that people are <u>selfish</u>, and <u>ignore inequalities</u> — as long as they benefit from them.

Poems can be About Aspects of Humanity

Love After Love (Pages 24-25)
1) This poem is about <u>being alone</u>.
2) The poet <u>challenges</u> the assumption that people are incomplete without <u>another person</u>.
3) The poet basically says you're often <u>better off on your own</u>. He advises the reader to "Give back your heart / To itself," as relationships can make you <u>betray your true identity</u>.

This Room (Pages 26-27)
1) The poem is about a <u>special moment</u> in life, when things suddenly <u>change for the better</u>.
2) We don't find out exactly what this moment is, and that adds to the universal feel of it — it stands for <u>any special, improbable event</u> in someone's life.
3) There's a sense of <u>optimism</u> about the poem — "This is the time and place / to be alive". The message is that you should <u>make the most</u> of opportunities when they come along.

Vultures (Pages 14-15)
1) It's about <u>good and evil</u>. The poet uses specific examples to move onto the topic in general.
2) Lines 22-29 are <u>universal</u>, and discuss how love and evil can exist separately in the same person.
3) Lines 41-51 are also universal, and sum up the theme of the poem. The poet asks whether we should be <u>grateful</u> that evil people are <u>capable of love</u>, or <u>depressed</u> because that love will always be <u>infected with evil</u>.

Specific examples can stand for things in general

Universal ideas are also dealt with in 'Nothing's Changed' (pages 4-5), 'Not my Business' (pages 30-31) and 'Hurricane Hits England' (32-33). The trick with this theme is to say how <u>specific situations</u> can be <u>applied to life in general</u>.

Section Two — The Themes

Traditions

A <u>tradition</u> is a belief or custom that's been <u>passed down</u> from one generation to the next.

> 1) Some poets use traditions as a <u>link</u> to their <u>culture</u>, <u>past</u> or <u>identity</u>.
> 2) Sometimes they <u>criticise</u> traditions, seeing them as just silly <u>superstitions</u>.
> 3) Traditions can seem <u>distant</u> and <u>mysterious</u>.

Some Traditions are *Mysterious*

Night of the Scorpion (Pages 12-13)

1) The poet describes traditional <u>Hindu</u> beliefs about <u>reincarnation</u>.
2) The villagers believe that the <u>pain</u> the boy's mother is feeling will mean her <u>next life</u> will be <u>better</u>.
3) The poet seems <u>separated</u> from this, probably because his dad isn't a Hindu believer. So these traditions appear <u>strange</u> and <u>superstitious</u> to him.
4) The poet's description of them calmly sitting in a <u>circle</u> around his mother, while she "twisted through and through", sounds <u>critical</u> — he wishes they would do something more <u>practical</u> to help her.

What Were They Like? (Pages 16-17)

1) The poem is about <u>Vietnamese</u> traditions and culture, written as though these are lost forever.
2) The descriptions of these traditions have an <u>uncertain</u> feel to them, to emphasise that the war has destroyed this culture and its traditions for ever.
3) There's a <u>mysterious but beautiful</u> feel to this way of life — "stone lanterns illumined pleasant ways". This adds to the poet's <u>anger</u> at what has happened to Vietnam.
4) But there are also questions about <u>ceremonies</u> and <u>ornaments</u>, showing that they had plenty <u>in common with us</u> too.
5) "It is not remembered" whether they had an "epic poem". <u>Traditional stories</u> usually last for a very long time, but even these have disappeared, showing that all <u>links to the past</u> have been <u>lost</u>.

Traditions can Provide a *Link with the Past*

Limbo (Pages 2-3)

1) The <u>limbo dance</u> originated from memories of being transported in cramped <u>slave ships</u>.
2) It's now a traditional <u>West Indian</u> dance that celebrates black people's <u>survival</u> and <u>freedom</u>.
3) The poet uses the "*limbo like me*" refrain to emphasise his <u>links with black history</u>.
4) Slave history and traditions are linked to his <u>freedom</u> at the end of the poem, when "the drummers are praising me" — his <u>solidarity</u> with the slaves helps him <u>break free</u>.

"Remind me, why are we doing this?"

Hurricane Hits England (Pages 32-33)

1) Traditional <u>African</u> beliefs say that the weather is caused by <u>gods</u>.
2) The poet calls on the <u>storm gods</u> (Huracan, Oya and Shango) to explain <u>why</u> the hurricane has come to England.
3) The poet uses these gods as a <u>link</u> with her <u>Caribbean roots</u>. She feels a new sense of <u>freedom</u> and <u>purpose</u>.

Traditions can be described positively or negatively

Traditions are also explored in Presents from my Aunts in Pakistan (pages 28-29). Most of the poets have pretty strong opinions about tradition and culture — they're generally either <u>well into it</u>, or they think it's <u>a bit silly</u>, even if they don't say so outright.

Section Two — The Themes

48 SECTION THREE — HOW TO ANSWER THE QUESTION

Sample Essay and Exam Method: Identity

FOLLOW THIS FIVE-STEP METHOD FOR A DECENT ANSWER EVERY TIME

First, the basics. You get 45 minutes for this question in the exam. It's crucial that you spend about 10 minutes of this planning your answer — if you don't, your essay will be a big pile of pants.

Remember — every question deals with a theme. The theme for this sample question is identity. Other key words in this question are "ideas" and "feelings". Refer to them throughout your essay. I've highlighted them in the sample answer on page 49.

1) Write a Bit About the Theme

1) Give a definition of the theme. You don't have to go into any detail — this example is quite basic.
2) Explain how the theme relates to the poems you will write about.

2) Compare the Structures of Each Poem

1) Say in one sentence how the structure of the two poems relates to the theme of the question.
2) Think about the "Structure" parts of the pages on each poem (pages 18-19 for 'Search...', and 28-29 for 'Presents...'). Use these to explain in more detail how the structure of the poems relates to the theme in the question. Write a couple of sentences about each poem.
3) Write about any similarities and differences in the structure of the two poems.
   You could write about some of these things, if any of them really stand out:

   - Line length
   - Stanza shape
   - Rhyme or rhythm
   - Repetition
   - Symmetry
   - Narrative or time-scale
   - Punctuation
   - Layout

3) Compare the Use of Language in Each Poem

1) Think about the "Language" parts of the pages on each poem (pages 18-19 for 'Search...', and 28-29 for 'Presents...').
2) For each poem, pick the type of fancy language that best relates to the theme. Then, for each poem, write a couple of sentences about how this type of fancy language relates to the theme of the question.
3) Explain any similarities and differences in the way that the two poets use language in their poems.
   You could include some of these things, if any of them really stand out:

   - Images, similes and metaphors
   - Who is speaking
   - Tone or atmosphere
   - Powerful words
   - Onomatopoeia
   - Alliteration
   - Assonance
   - Personification
   - Non-standard English
   - Contrasting ideas between poems
   - Questions or commands

4) Compare the Feelings of the Poets

1) Write one sentence about how the feelings of the poets are similar or different. Relate it to the theme of the question.
2) Look at the "Poet's Feelings and Attitudes" parts of the poem pages. Pick the ones that relate best to the theme of the question. Write about the similarities and differences between the two poems.

5) Write About How the Poems Make you Feel

1) Say which poem you preferred and why.
2) Say what you've learnt about the theme.
3) Show some empathy — connect the poem to your own feelings and experiences.

Section Three — How to Answer the Question

Sample Essay and Exam Method: Identity

THIS SAMPLE ESSAY USES THE FIVE-STEP METHOD

Learn the stuff on your poems and themes, then use this method in the exam, and you'll be fine.

> **Question 1** Compare 'Presents from my Aunts in Pakistan' with one other poem, showing how the poets reveal **ideas** and **feelings** about their **identity**.

Our age, our gender, our social position and our personality make up our **identity**. Where we come from can also have a strong influence: the country or regions in which we grow up and live can have an important impact on how we see ourselves. In 'Search for my Tongue', it is language that is central to **identity**, whereas in 'Presents from my Aunts in Pakistan', dress and family customs are important ideas.

— Talk about the theme straight away — that's what the question is about.

The poets structure their poems in different ways to express their **ideas** and **feelings** about **identity**. 'Search...' has a clear, three part layout which shows the poet's **feelings** about her divided **identity**. The difficulties of being fluent in two languages are explained in lines 1-16. Lines 17-30, in Gujarati (with phonetic spelling), describe how the mother tongue returns during her dreams and lines 31-39 are a "translation" of the Gujarati. This structure shows us the problem of **identity** for the poet, as she has put the Gujarati tongue at the heart of the poem as it is at the heart of her being. In contrast, 'Presents...' has a very haphazard structure with varied line lengths and layout, reflecting the teenage girl's confusion over her **identity**.

— Make sure you constantly refer to the key words in the question — I've highlighted them.

Metaphorical language is used in both poems to show the poets' **ideas** about **identity**. For instance, in 'Search...' there is an extended metaphor of the tongues being like plants growing in her mouth, with her mother tongue eventually dominating: it "grows longer, grows moist, grows strong veins, it ties the other tongue in knots". This metaphor emphasises her **feelings** about her **identity** coming through her mother tongue. In "Presents..." the image of the snapped bangles suggests the girl wants to break free of her Pakistani **identity**. The fact that the bangles drew blood suggests how painful, physically and mentally, her torn identity is. The young girl in "Presents..." seems to want to escape from her cultural roots but, in contrast, Sujata Bhatt is delighted when her mother tongue returns.

— Remember — you've got to compare and contrast the two poems all the time.

There are both similarities and differences in the ways that the poets use language to show their **feelings** about their **identity**. Both poets show regret at not having a clear sense of who they are or where they belong. The teenage girl in 'Presents...' tries on the Pakistani clothes but **feels** "alien in the sitting room. I could never be as lovely as those clothes". The word "alien" is particularly effective in expressing how unnatural and unhappy she feels. Similarly, Bhatt asks the reader to imagine the conflict between her two languages: "You could not use them both together". They also share the **feelings** of wanting to know their "real" self. Bhatt is pleased when she realises, "Everytime I think I've forgotten, I think I've lost the mother tongue, it blossoms out of my mouth". However, in 'Presents...' the girl longs "for denim and corduroy" and realises she is "half-English, unlike Aunt Jamila". The **feelings** each poet expresses about their **identity** have a link in that they both are uncertain about who they are, and regret the loss of their cultural roots. The difference is that in 'Search...' the woman's mother tongue returns to her and she feels happy: "it blossoms out of my mouth", but in 'Presents...' the girl doesn't feel completely comfortable in either her English or her Pakistani **identity**.

I enjoyed both these poems, but I preferred 'Presents...' as I feel it is easier to relate to the **feelings** in this poem. The way Sujata Bhatt discusses **identity** is quite specific, and difficult to relate to unless the reader also speaks two languages. I think that Moniza Alvi's description of the confusion of trying to work out who you really are, on the other hand, is a feeling that many of us can relate to, regardless of our background.

— You've got to write about your feelings towards the poems. Don't worry if you don't feel anything — just write something believable.

Section Three — How to Answer the Question

Sample Essay and Exam Method: Description

THIS FIVE-STEP METHOD IS GOOD FOR A TOP-NOTCH ANSWER EVERY TIME

First, the basics. You get 45 minutes for this question in the exam. It's crucial that you spend about 10 minutes of this planning your answer — if you don't, your essay will be complete and utter rubbish.

Remember — every question deals with a theme. The theme for this sample question is description. Other key words in this question are "thoughts" and "feelings". Refer to them throughout your essay. I've highlighted them in the sample essay on the next page.

1) Write a Bit About the Theme

1) Give a definition. You don't have to go into any detail — this example is quite straightforward.
2) Explain how the theme is used in the poems you will write about.

2) Compare the Structures of Each Poem

1) Say in one sentence how the structure of the two poems relates to the theme of the question.
2) Think about the "Structure" parts of the pages on each poem (pages 4-5 for 'Nothing's Changed', and 8-9 for 'Blessing'). Use these to explain in more detail how the structure of the poems relates to the theme in the question. Write a couple of sentences about each poem.
3) Write about the similarities and differences in the structure of the two poems.
   You could write about some of these things, if any of them really stand out:

   - Line length
   - Stanza shape
   - Rhyme or rhythm
   - Repetition
   - Symmetry
   - Narrative or time-scale
   - Punctuation
   - Layout

3) Compare the Use of Language in Each Poem

1) Look at the "Language" parts of the pages on each poem (pages 4-5 for 'Nothing's Changed', and 8-9 for 'Blessing').
2) For each poem, pick the type of fancy language that best relates to the theme. Then, for each poem, write a few sentences about how this type of fancy language relates to the theme of the question.
3) Explain the similarities and differences in the way that the two poets use language in their poems.
   You could include some of these things, if any of them really stand out:

   - Images, similes and metaphors
   - Who is speaking
   - Tone or atmosphere
   - Powerful words
   - Onomatopoeia
   - Alliteration
   - Assonance
   - Personification
   - Non-standard English
   - Contrasting ideas between poems
   - Questions and commands

4) Compare the Feelings of the Poets

1) Write one sentence about how the feelings of the poets are similar or different. Relate it to the theme of the question.
2) Look at the "Poet's Feelings and Attitudes" parts of the poem pages. Pick the ones that relate best to the theme of the question. Write about the similarities and differences between the two poems.

5) Write About How the Poems Make you Feel

1) Say which poem you preferred and why.
2) Say what you've learnt about the theme.
3) Show some empathy — connect the poem to your own feelings and experiences.

Section Three — How to Answer the Question

Sample Essay and Exam Method: Description

HERE'S ANOTHER EXAMPLE OF THE FIVE-STEP METHOD

Practise using this method to make sure you're ready for the Exam.

> **Question 2** — Compare 'Nothing's Changed' with one other poem, showing how poets use description to convey their thoughts and feelings in their poems.

Description is a useful technique for poets to use as it enables the reader to visualise and understand the themes and ideas of a piece more clearly. In 'Nothing's Changed', description makes us realise the significance of District Six for this poet. In 'Blessing', descriptive techniques are used differently in order to recreate the people's feelings and actions, as well as creating a picture of their environment.

It's good to use the key words from the question because it shows that you are answering it directly.

The structure of 'Nothing's Changed' is based around the poet's return to District Six, and the descriptions are vital to our understanding of this event. As he walks through the area he recognises it instinctively but then is shocked by the "whites only inn". He becomes angry as he is effectively forced to go to the "working man's cafe", and this makes him remember all the past injustices. The structure of "Blessing" has a role in supporting the description. The four stanzas describe different aspects of the event. The descriptions in lines 12 to 23 are listed one after another, adding to the sense of the desperate action, as the villagers rush to collect the water with their "frantic hands". Reading the first and last lines of the poem together gives the disturbing simile, "The skin cracks like a pod/over their small bones".

Try and write a similar amount about each poem — this'll make sure that your answer is balanced.

There are many different descriptive devices used in both poems, and these emphasise the poets' thoughts and feelings about their subjects. 'Nothing's Changed' starts by using alliteration and onomatopoeia in short, harsh words such as "cuffs, cans" and "crunch". These words show the poet's feeling of brewing anger as well as the environment. The simile used to describe the hotel, "name flaring like a flag," reveals the arrogance of the white establishment. The images of glass describe a range of ideas: it is a barrier keeping him out — "I press my nose to the clear panes"; it represents the white class drinking — "crushed ice, white glass"; it reflects him as a "boy again"; and finally it is used to describe his intention to strike back, to "shiver down the glass" and all that it represents.

Using terms like onomatopoeia is ace — it helps you to explain what you mean without waffling.

In "Blessing", methods of description are important to our understanding of the reactions of the local people to the burst pipe, their living conditions and how highly they value water. The simile, "The skin cracks like a pod", brings home the dryness. A sense of bustle is created when we hear, "a roar of tongues", as they shout and scream with delight at the sudden provision of water. Metaphors like "fortune" and "silver" are used to describe the value they put on water. The phrase "liquid sun" suggests its life-giving quality. These descriptions are most powerful when linked to their religion; there is "a congregation", who worship a "small splash" as "the voice of a kindly god". The poet clearly feels respect and admiration this community for their attitude to life in such difficult conditions.

There is a real difference in the description of the thoughts and feelings expressed in these two poems. The poet in 'Nothing's Changed' is very much at the centre of the poem. The negative feelings of anger and bitter disappointment he describes here are very much his own, the "inward turning anger of my eyes." In contrast, 'Blessing' describes the celebratory thoughts and feelings of a group of people, "naked children screaming in the liquid sun," as well as the understated concern and respect that the poet feels for them.

I found 'Nothing's Changed' more interesting than 'Blessing' because of the historical and political aspects. I have been impressed by how descriptive techniques used in poems like this can effectively recreate the different environments and also convey the thoughts and feelings of the poets. These poems have made me realise how fortunate I am in living in this country, where water is plentiful, and we can enjoy freedom and equality.

It looks good if you can relate the issues in the poem to your life — it shows that you appreciate what the poet is feeling.

Section Three — How to Answer the Question

Sample Essay and Exam Method: Politics

FOR A SUREFIRE QUALITY ANSWER, FOLLOW THE FIVE-STEP METHOD

First, the basics. You get 45 minutes for this question in the exam. It's crucial that you spend about 10 minutes of this planning your answer — if you don't, your essay will be drivel.

Remember — every question deals with a theme. The theme for this sample question is society. Other key words in this question are "attitudes" and "feelings". Refer to them throughout your essay. I've highlighted them in the sample essay on the next page.

1) Write a Bit About the Theme

1) Give a definition. You don't have to go into lots of detail — this example is pretty simple.
2) Explain how the theme is used in the poems you will write about.

2) Compare the Structures of Each Poem

1) Say in one sentence how the structure of the two poems relates to the theme of the question.
2) Think about the "Structure" parts of the pages on each poem (pages 30-31 for 'Not my Business', and 20-21 for 'Unrelated Incidents'). Use these to explain in more detail about how the structure of the poems relates to the theme in the question. Write a couple of sentences about each poem.
3) Write about the similarities and differences in the structure of the two poems.

You could write about some of these things, if any of them really stand out:

- Line length
- Rhyme or rhythm
- Symmetry
- Punctuation
- Stanza shape
- Repetition
- Narrative or time-scale
- Layout

3) Compare the Use of Language in Each Poem

1) Look at the "Language" parts of the pages on each poem (pages 30-31 for 'Not my Business', and 20-21 for 'Unrelated Incidents').
2) For each poem, pick the type of fancy language that best relates to the theme. Then, for each poem, write a couple of sentences about how this type of fancy language relates to the theme of the question.
3) Explain the similarities and differences in the way that the two poets use language in their poems.

You could include some of these things, if any of them really stand out:

- Images, similes and metaphors
- Powerful words
- Assonance
- Contrasting ideas between poems
- Who is speaking
- Onomatopoeia
- Personification
- Questions or commands
- Tone or atmosphere
- Alliteration
- Non-standard English

4) Compare the Feelings of the Poets

1) Write one sentence about how the feelings of the poets are similar or different. Relate it to the theme of the question.
2) Look at the "Poet's Feelings and Attitudes" parts of the poem pages. Pick the ones that relate best to the theme of the question. Write about the similarities and differences between the two poems.

5) Write About How the Poems Make you Feel

1) Say which poem you preferred and why.
2) Say what you've learnt about the theme.
3) Show some empathy — connect the poem to your own feelings and experiences.

Section Three — How to Answer the Question

Sample Essay and Exam Method: Politics

THE FIVE-STEP METHOD IS SIMPLE TO USE

Here's another example of how to use the five-step method.

Question 3 — Compare 'Not my Business' with one other poem which demonstrates strong attitudes and feelings about how individuals are treated in society.

The political organisation of a country is not just about the type of government it has; it also involves how people in communities relate to each other. The UK is a democracy where rights are protected and everyone is considered equal, but some countries are dictatorships where people fear losing their freedom and even their lives.

It's good to show that you understand the political circumstances that the poet is writing about.

In 'Not my Business', we hear the voice of an individual whose attitude is that it is best to stay out of politics. However, the poet's view is that everyone should be involved, otherwise people will end up being treated cruelly. 'Unrelated Incidents' is about people's attitudes towards language. It is about how British newsreaders usually talk in upper class, English accents, and how in our society this accent is associated with power and authority. The poem highlights how people's voices and points of view can be marginalised if they speak in a working-class or regional accent.

Both poets use structure to convey their attitudes and feelings. The four stanzas of 'Not my Business' follow a narrative structure. Each stanza provides a different example of the brutality of the regime, "They picked Akanni up one morning / Beat him soft like clay". The first three stanzas have repeated lines at the end; in these lines, instead of facing up to the cruel treatment of his friends, he asks, "What business of mine is it?" A pattern is established by the times of day referenced in each stanza, "They came one night...And then one evening". This shows that these people are never safe, whether it is day or night. In contrast, 'Unrelated Incidents' has a simple but unusual layout. It resembles a newsreader's autocue, so it relates to the subject. The short lines are startling but are used to make the poet's point about how regional dialects are not acceptable as carriers of the news, "yi / widny wahnt / mi ti talk / aboot thi / trooth wia / voice lik / wanna yoo / scruff". However, the short lines make it appear as if he is mocking "normal language".

Make sure you include quotes to back up the points you are making.

The way that poetic devices are used in the poems differs. 'Not my Business' uses a range of techniques to emphasise the attitudes and feelings in the poem. The threat of violence is a constant theme. In the first stanza the simile describes how Akanni's body changes shape due to the beating. The metaphor that follows, "stuffed him down the belly / Of a waiting jeep," reinforces the idea of the regime being like a vicious predator. The use of personification in "bewildered lawn" suggests that even the country's landscape is affected by the regime's brutality. It shows how it is inescapable and maybe undefeatable. In contrast, the poetic devices used in 'Unrelated Incidents' are limited. The lack of punctuation and capital letters reinforces the poet's attempt to make fun of BBC English. The phonetic spelling is the most obvious device, which wittily allows us to try out his dialect and hear the ironic message he puts across: "thirza right / way ti spell / ana right way / ti tok it". He feels strongly that the educated, English middle classes hold power and exercise it through the way they speak. Their message to him and people like him is clear: "belt up".

Make suggestions about why you think the poet has chosen to use particular poetic devices.

There are strong attitudes and feelings in both poems. Both poets express anger at the situations they describe. Osundare is not only angry at corrupt regimes, but also at the complacent attitudes of people who try and hide from such issues in society. The title is clearly ironic: it should be our business. Similarly, Tom Leonard is angry with the way people with local accents and dialects are seen as inferior to those who speak "correctly". We also sense the feelings of the characters in both poems. The man is obviously terrified that he will be taken next and experiences the guilt of inaction, whereas the "scruffs" in Leonard's poem feel inadequate and powerless because of society's attitude to how they speak.

I think it is important that people recognise and react to the inequalities in the way people are treated in society. 'Not my Business' demonstrates that people have a responsibility to protect and care about each other's rights. If we ignore abuses and inequalities they can become more widespread. British society can appear to be much fairer than the society described in 'Not my Business'. However, Tom Leonard's poem shows that inequalities do exist, such as the predominance of English, middle class (BBC) accents as the voices of power and authority.

Summarise the main points that you have made in your essay to draw everything to a conclusion.

Section Three — How to Answer the Question

Sample Essay and Exam Method: People

FOLLOW THIS FIVE-STEP METHOD FOR A DECENT ANSWER EVERY TIME

First, the basics. You get <u>45 minutes</u> for this question in the exam. It's <u>crucial</u> that you spend about <u>10 minutes</u> of this <u>planning</u> your answer — if you don't, your essay will be scuppered from the start.

Remember — <u>every question</u> deals with a theme. The theme for this sample question is <u>people</u>. Other <u>key words</u> in this question are "<u>conflict</u>" and "<u>cultures</u>". Refer to them throughout your essay. I've highlighted them in the sample essay on the next page.

1) Write a Bit About the Theme

1) Give a <u>definition</u>. It doesn't have to be technical — just describe what you think the theme means.
2) <u>Explain</u> how the theme is explored in the poems you will write about.

2) Compare the Structures of Each Poem

1) Say in <u>one sentence</u> how the structure of the two poems <u>relates to the theme of the question</u>.
2) Think about the "<u>Structure</u>" parts of the pages on each poem (pages 6-7 for 'Island Man', and 10-11 for 'Two Scavengers...'). Use these to write about how the <u>structure</u> of the poems <u>relates</u> to the <u>theme in the question</u>. Write a <u>couple of sentences</u> about each poem.
3) Write about the <u>similarities</u> and <u>differences</u> in the structure of the two poems. You could write about some of these things, if any of them <u>really stand out</u>:

- Line length
- Rhyme or rhythm
- Symmetry
- Punctuation
- Stanza shape
- Repetition
- Narrative or time-scale
- Layout

3) Compare the Use of Language in Each Poem

1) Look at the "<u>Language</u>" parts of the pages on each poem (pages 6-7 for 'Island Man', and 10-11 for 'Two Scavengers...').
2) For each poem, pick the <u>type of fancy language</u> that <u>best relates to the theme</u>. Then, for <u>each</u> poem, write a couple of sentences about <u>how</u> this type of fancy language relates to the theme of the question.
3) Explain the <u>similarities</u> and <u>differences</u> in the way that the two poets use language in their poems. You could include some of these things, if any of them really stand out:

- Images, similes and metaphors
- Powerful words
- Assonance
- Contrasting ideas between poems
- Who is speaking
- Onomatopoeia
- Personification
- Questions or commands
- Tone or atmosphere
- Alliteration
- Non-standard English

4) Compare the Feelings of the Poets

1) Write <u>one sentence</u> about how the <u>feelings</u> of the poets are <u>similar or different</u>. Relate it to the <u>theme of the question</u>.
2) Look at the "<u>Poet's Feelings and Attitudes</u>" parts of the poem pages. Pick the ones that <u>relate best</u> to the theme of the question. Write about the <u>similarities and differences</u> between the two poems.

5) Write About How the Poems Make you Feel

1) Say which poem you <u>preferred</u> and <u>why</u>.
2) Say what you've <u>learnt</u> about the theme.
3) Show some <u>empathy</u> — connect the poem to <u>your own feelings and experiences</u>.

Section Three — How to Answer the Question

Sample Essay and Exam Method: People

YOU CAN USE THE FIVE-STEP METHOD FOR ANY QUESTION

Here's one more example for you to have a look at.

> **Question 4**   Compare 'Island Man' with one other poem, to show how the poets use people to explain the conflict that can exist between and within different cultures.

People are at the centre all communities. They embody the values, customs and ideas that a particular culture possesses. By examining how people behave and think, it is possible to gain a greater understanding of how their cultural roots affect them. 'Island Man' describes how an immigrant in London reacts to his environment as he dreams of his Caribbean home. In contrast, the people in 'Two Scavengers...' all live in San Francisco, but lead totally different lives there.

Try to establish why the theme is important in your opening paragraph.

'Island Man' uses structure to show the conflicting and confused waking thoughts of the man. There is no punctuation, the line lengths vary and some phrases are totally misplaced, as is the individual: "he always comes back   groggily groggily". Like 'Island Man', 'Two Scavengers...' also has no punctuation. It represents an instant in time, like the flash of a camera. The conflicting images seem to be laid one on top of the other, line by line, emphasising the contrasts between the two lifestyles.

Talk about the methods that the poets use to explore the themes.

The language in 'Island Man' shows the inner turmoil that the character is going through. The reader gets a series of contrasting images. For example, "the sound of the blue surf" of the Caribbean conflicts with, the "grey metallic soar" of London. The "pillow waves" show the troubled sleep he has had which has caused the ruffles, but also tells of the dreams he has had of his "emerald island". The word "wombing" suggests the sense of security his homeland offers him, in contrast to the faceless "dull North Circular roar" of London. Contrast is also used in 'Two Scavengers...', but here it is the contrast of the different types of people: the woman is "casually coifed", the older man is "grungy". Although the young men's hair and glasses are similar, their appearances are mostly very different; the "hip three-piece linen suit" conflicts with the "red plastic blazers".

It will impress the Examiner if you can show that you empathise with the characters in the poem.

The use of vocabulary is effective in both poems. Some words, such as "soar", "roar" and "surge" have double meanings: they are positive when they relate to his island, but have negative meanings in London. In 'Two Scavengers...', descriptive words are used to highlight the differences between the people. For example, "scavengers" are unworthy compared to "an elegant couple". The poet uses this contrast to make a direct criticism of society and how it creates this division between rich and poor people. Phrases like "small gulf" emphasise how these people may only be a few metres apart on the street, but, in terms of their lifestyles, they will never meet.

Both poets show how the people feel in their different situations and give us their own view. 'Island Man' obviously has fond memories of the Caribbean but resents his dull lifestyle in London. We can feel his depression as he "heaves himself" to "Another London day". Grace Nichols has sympathy for this man as he feels the conflict of these two cultures. The feelings revealed in 'Two Scavengers...' are very one-sided, as we have the envy of the poor, "as if they were watching some odorless TV ad / in which everything is always possible," contrasting with the uncaring attitude of the rich, who don't even seem to notice the truck or its passengers. The poet's attitude here is one of despair at this unequal society.

'Island Man' has made me more aware how it might feel to be trapped in a foreign country, while 'Two Scavengers...' starkly highlights the divisions in American society. The poems have made me hope that in the future, society will be more equal and that governments who promise equal opportunities for all will deliver on what they say.

Try and work out what comment on society the author is trying to make through their poem.

Section Three — How to Answer the Question

Glossary

accent	The way people pronouce words. It can vary between different countries, regions and social backgrounds.
alliteration	Where consonants are repeated. It's often used in poetry to give a nice pattern to a phrase. E.g. 'Sally's slipper slipped on a slimy slug.'
assonance	When words share the same vowel sound, but the consonants are different. E.g. "Lisa had a piece of cheese before she went to sleep, to help her dream."
consonants	All the letters in the alphabet that aren't vowels.
contrast	When two things are described in a way which emphasises how different they are. E.g. a poet might contrast two different places, or two different cultures.
dialect	Regional variation of a language. People from different places might use different words or different sentence constructions. E.g. In some northern English dialects, people might say "Ey up" instead of "Hello".
empathy	When someone feels like they understand what someone else is experiencing and how they feel about it.
imagery	Language that creates a picture in your mind, bringing the text to life.
language	The choice of words used. The language determines the effect the piece of writing will have on the reader, e.g. it can be emotive or persuasive.
layout	The way a piece of writing is visually presented to the reader. E.g. what kind of font is used, whether there are sub-headings and bullet points, how the verses in a poem are broken up, whether sentences or lines are arranged regularly, whether they create some kind of visual pattern, etc.
metaphor	A way of describing something by saying that it is something else, to create a vivid image. E.g. "His eyes were deep, black, oily pools."
narrator	The voice speaking the words that you're reading. E.g. a poem could be written from the point of view of a young child, which means the young child is the poem's narrator.
non-standard	Any form of English that isn't 'proper' English. Things like slang, phonetic spelling and dialect are all examples of non-standard English.
onomatopoeia	A word that sounds like what it's supposed to mean. E.g. "buzz", "crunch", "bang", "pop", "ding".
personification	A special kind of metaphor where you write about something as if it's a person with thoughts and feelings. E.g. "The sea growled hungrily."

Glossary

phonetic	When words are spelt as they sound rather than with their usual spelling. It's often used to show that someone's speaking with a certain accent.
pun	A "play on words" — a word or phrase that's deliberately used because it has more than one meaning. E.g. "She lies on the couch at the psychiatrist's", where "lies" could mean "lies down" or "tells lies".
repetition	Obvious really — where a word or phrase is repeated to emphasise a point or idea.
rhythm	When sentences or lines have a fixed pattern of syllables. It's often used in poetry.
simile	A way of describing something by comparing it to something else, usually by using the words "like" or "as". E.g. "He was as pale as the moon," or "Her hair was like a bird's nest."
stanza	A group of lines in a poem that usually share the same rhythm pattern and similar line lengths. Stanzas can also be called verses.
stereotype	An inaccurate, generalised view of a particular group of people. E.g. A stereotype of football fans might be that they're all hooligans.
structure	The order a piece of writing is arranged in. E.g. how the poem begins, develops and ends, whether it uses verses or not, whether it has a particular layout, etc.
syllable	A single unit of sound within a word. E.g. "all" has one syllable, "always" has two and "establishmentarianism" has nine.
symbolism	When an object stands for something else. E.g. a candle might be a symbol of hope, or a dying flower could symbolise the end of a relationship.
theme	An idea or topic that's important in a piece of writing. E.g. a poem could be based on the theme of friendship.
tone	The mood of a piece of writing, e.g. happy, sad, serious, lighthearted. It's an overall effect, created by things like choice of words, imagery and layout.
voice	The personality narrating the poem. Poems are usually written either using the poet's voice, as if they're speaking to you directly, or the voice of a character, e.g. an elderly man, or a horse.
vowels	Simple — the letters 'a', 'e', 'i', 'o' and 'u' and sometimes 'y'.

Index

A
accent 20, 21, 43
Africa 3, 34, 39, 47
alliteration 2, 4
America 39, 44
apartheid 4, 5, 34, 36
argumentative tone 23
assonance 18

B
bitterness 5
'Blessing' 8, 9, 40, 41, 50, 51

C
Caribbean 3, 6, 7, 23, 32-34, 39, 40, 43, 44, 47
celebration 24
ceremonial language 25
ceremony 12
change 5, 17, 36
Chinua Achebe 14, 15
Christianity 24
colonies 3
comparison 5, 11
conflict 18, 19, 29
contemplative tone 15
contradiction 10
contrast 4, 29
conversational language 19
conversational tone 18, 22, 38
creole 23, 43
culture 16, 17, 19, 42, 45, 47

D
democracy 10, 35, 39, 44
Denise Levertov 16, 17
Derek Walcott 24, 25
description 7, 40, 50
devastation 17
dialect 21, 34, 43

District Six 4, 5, 36, 39, 40
double meanings 2, 7, 18

E
Edward Kamau Brathwaite 2, 3
enlightenment 32
equality 46
essays 49, 51, 53, 55
exam questions 48-55

F
factual tone 13
first person 13, 32, 38
foreign language 19
formal tone 17

G
gods 33
government 35
Grace Nichols 6, 7, 32, 33
Gujarati 18, 19, 34, 36, 41, 42, 45

H
'Half-Caste' 22, 23, 37, 41, 43, 45, 46
Hinduism 12, 13, 39, 47
home 33
homeland 32
humanity 46
humour 23, 41
'Hurricane Hits England' 32-34, 37, 39, 44, 45, 47

I
identity 19, 28, 29, 34, 44, 48, 49
improbability 27
Imtiaz Dharker 8, 9, 26, 27
India 18

indignation 33
inequality 5, 38
instructive language 25
irony 43
irregular rhyme scheme 8
irregular structure 7
Islam 8
'Island Man' 6, 7, 37, 40, 43, 54, 55

J
John Agard 22, 23
joke 22

L
language 7, 9, 17, 19, 34, 48
Lawrence Ferlinghetti 10, 11
legend 28
'Limbo' 2, 3, 39, 42, 43, 47
London 6, 37, 40
'Love After Love' 24, 25, 46

M
memory 29
metaphor 3, 5, 9, 15, 17, 18, 19, 23, 29, 32, 41
mockery 41
Moniza Alvi 28, 29
mood 14
mother tongue 18, 19, 34, 36, 41
mythical language 33

N
narrative 31
nature 33
negativity 24
Nelson Mandela 5
'Night of the Scorpion' 12, 13, 38, 39, 47

Index

Nissim Ezekiel 12, 13
Niyi Osundare 30, 31
non-standard English 43
'Not my Business' 30,
    31, 37, 38, 52, 53
'Nothing's Changed' 4,
    5, 34, 35, 36,
    38-40, 44, 50, 51

O

onomatopoeia 4
opposition 45

P

pain 29
Pakistan 8, 28, 29, 45
particular places 44
people 40, 54
personification 14, 26, 27,
    30, 32
philosophical language 33
phonetic spelling 21, 43
places 40
politics 21, 35, 36,
    52, 53
'Presents from my Aunts in
    Pakistan' 28, 29,
    34, 36, 38, 40,
    44, 45, 48, 49

R

refrain 30, 31, 47
reincarnation 12, 13,
    39, 47
religion 8, 13, 25, 32,
    34, 38
repetition 2, 3, 4, 10, 18
resentment 7
respectful language 17
rhyme 22
rhythm 2, 3

S

San Francisco 11
sarcasm 21
'Search For My Tongue'
    18, 19, 34, 36, 38,
    41, 42, 45, 48, 49
segregation 4, 39, 44
similes 4, 41
slavery 3, 39, 43
social commentary 11
solitude 46
South Africa 5, 35,
    39, 44
specific cultural references
    39
speech marks 20
structure 7, 48
Sujata Bhatt 18, 19
superstition 38
surreal images 38
syllable 2
symbolism 2, 12, 15

T

Tatamkhulu Afrika 4, 5
'This Room' 26, 27, 36,
    38, 41, 46
Tom Leonard 20, 21
tone 9, 13, 14, 22, 38
traditions 47
two cultures 29, 45
'Two Scavengers in a Truck...'
    10, 11, 35, 37,
    39, 40, 44, 46,
    54, 55

U

uncertainty 29
universal ideas 46
'Unrelated Incidents'
    20, 21, 34, 35,
    42, 43, 45, 52, 53
unusual presentation 42

V

Vietnam 16, 17, 35,
    36, 42, 47
violence 31
visual contrast 18
'Vultures' 14, 15, 35, 41,
    44, 46

W

way of life 17
'What Were They Like?'
    16, 17, 35, 42, 47

Acknowledgements

The Publisher would like to thank:

Chinua Achebe 'Vultures' from *Beware Soul Brother* (African Writers, Heinemann Educational, 1972)

Tatamkhulu Afrika 'Nothing's Changed' © Tatamkhulu Afrika

John Agard 'Half Caste' reproduced by kind permission of John Agard c/o Caroline Sheldon Literary Agency from *Get Back Pimple* (Penguin, 1996).

Moniza Alvi *Carrying My Wife*, Bloodaxe Books, 2000

Sujata Bhatt 'Search for My Tongue' from *Brunizem* (1998), reprinted by permission of the publishers, Carcanet Press Ltd.

Edward Kamau Brathwaite 'Limbo' from *The Arrivants: A New World Trilogy* (OUP, 1973), reprinted by permission of Oxford University Press.

Imtiaz Dharker *Postcards from god*, Bloodaxe Books, 1997; *I Speak for the Devil*, Bloodaxe Books 2001

Nissim Ezekiel 'Night of the Scorpion' from *Poverty Poems*, reproduced by permission of Oxford University Press India, New Delhi

Lawrence Ferlinghetti 'Two Scavengers in A Truck, Two Beautiful People In A Mercedes' from *These Are My Rivers*, copyright © 1979 by Lawrence Ferlinghetti. Reprinted by permission of New Directions Publishing Corp.

Tom Leonard 'Unrelated Incidents' © Tom Leonard, from *Intimate Voices* Etruscan Books, Devon

Denise Levertov 'What Were They Like?' from *Selected Poems* (Bloodaxe Books, 1986). Reproduced by permission of Pollinger Limited and the proprietor.

Grace Nichols 'Island Man' from *The Fat Black Woman's Poems* (Virago, 1984), copyright © Grace Nichols 1984, and 'Hurricane Hits England' from *Sunrise* (Virago, 1996), copyright © Grace Nichols 1996

Niyi Osundare 'Not My Business' from *Songs of the Seasons* © Niyi Osundare (Heinemann Educational Books, Nigeria, 1990)

Derek Walcott 'Love After Love' from *Collected Poems 1948-1984* (1986), Faber and Faber

Photographs:

Photograph of Grace Nichols © Sheila Geraghty
Photograph of Tom Leonard © Gordon Wright
Photograph of Denise Levertov © David Geier, courtesy of New Directions
Photograph of Moniza Alvi © Bob Coe
Photograph of Tatamkhulu Afrika Still frame taken from Devon Curriculum Services video, Tatamkhulu Afrika, District 6
Mansell Collection 'Plan of slaves crammed into one deck on a slaveship, the Brookes of Liverpool'

Every effort has been made to locate copyright holders and obtain permission to reproduce sources. For those sources where it has been difficult to trace the originator of the work, we would be grateful for information. If any copyright holder would like us to make an amendment to the acknowledgements, please notify us and we will gladly update the book at the next reprint. Thank you.